COUNSELING AND DEVELOPMENT SERIES
ALLEN IVEY, EDITOR

GILI'S BOOK
A Journey into Bereavement for Parents and Counselors
Henya Kagan (Klein)

CONSTRUCTIVIST THINKING IN
COUNSELING PRACTICE, RESEARCH, AND TRAINING
Thomas L. Sexton & Barbara L. Griffin, Editors

RESEARCH AS PRAXIS
Lessons from Programmatic
Research in Therapeutic Psychology
Lisa Tsoi Hoshmand & Jack Martin, Editors

THE CONSTRUCTION
AND UNDERSTANDING OF
PSYCHOTHERAPEUTIC CHANGE
Conversations, Memories, and Theories
Jack Martin

GILI'S BOOK

*A Journey Into Bereavement
for Parents and Families*

Henya Kagan (Klein)

Teachers College, Columbia University
New York and London

Published by Teachers College Press, 1234 Amsterdam Avenue, New York, NY 10027

Library of Congress Cataloging-in-Publication Data

Kagan, Henya.
   Gili's book : a journey into bereavement for parents and
  counselors / Henya Kagan (Klein).
     p. cm. — (Counseling and development series)
   Includes bibliographical references and index.
   ISBN 0-8077-3747-X (hardcover : alk. paper). ISBN 0-8077-3746-1 (pbk. : alk. paper)
   1. Grief. 2. Bereavement—Psychological aspects. 3. Children—
Death—Psychological aspects. 4. Loss (Psychology) I. Title.
II. Series.
BF575.G7K34   1998
155.9'37'092—dc21   98-17902

ISBN 0-8077-3746-1 (paper)
ISBN 0-8077-3747-X (cloth)

Printed on acid-free paper

Manufactured in the United States of America

05 04 03 02 01 00 99 98 8 7 6 5 4 3 2 1

Contents

Foreword

"Parental mourning is a natural reaction to an abnormal event."
—Henya Kagan (Klein)

Passed away, departed, deceased, on to another world—dead. We use many words and euphemisms to describe a painful reality of daily life. The act of naming deeply affects how we understand and cope with the world around us.

Elizabeth Kübler-Ross has been helpful to us with the stages of death and dying. She has enabled us to understand some of death's mysteries. Through the names denial, anger, bargaining, depression, and acceptance, she has eased the transition of death for many. Yet, out of her work new questions have arisen. The literature on death and dying is growing large. Not all of us who mourn experience her stages, nor those of other theorists; cultural differences in response to loss vary greatly and, to some bereaved individuals, the stages and theories seem irrelevant. How do we make sense of theoretical confusion?

Henya Kagan (Klein) comes to us with a new vision of death based on her profound personal experience with the sudden loss of her daughter, Gili, who died at the age of eleven. This book is a memorial to Gili. It is a book which will make many of us cry with the hurt and suffering we experience as we read these pages. At the same time, you will find a triumph in the joys and memories of a young life and a mother's love.

You will also come to reflect differently on our psychological theories of death and dying. The holistic meaning of the experience of loss is elegantly presented here in a manner which adds considerably to our psychological knowledge.

Henya Kagan (Klein) reminds us that each of us reacts differently to loss. While for some the initial response may indeed be denial, this mother and psychologist "looked straight into the eye of horror." Her experience is not our experience, but her directness and openness is rare. I learn about myself when I see the world through Henya's eyes and believe that you will as well.

This book leads us to question the concepts of "recovery" and "acceptance." How does one ever recover from the loss of a child, to say nothing of "accepting" it? The hurt and grief inside is always there. In that sense Henya presents what some might call an existential approach to death with an emphasis on uniqueness, holism, and the continuity of experience.

"I knew right away Gili was dead. . . . I never 'accepted' her death." We cannot and perhaps should not resolve our loss. Readjustment may be a wiser and more fruitful goal. It may be stronger and more honoring of the person whom we have lost to continue their lives in us. With them, we can build a new life for the present and the future.

It is only in the experience of the full anguish of loss that we really encounter life. This author reminds us that a survival mentality may be useful, but it is not living; nor does it honor the dead. Our emotional, physical, and spiritual task is to empower ourselves and to find a mission—to make meaning from the loss.

We need never stop our interactions with the deceased. This does not mean a morbid preoccupation. Rather it means we do not have to "let go" and we can continue to work through our issues with those who are deceased; for let us recall that few of us have "perfect" relationships with even those who are most loved. We also can treasure our memories and use these to build new understandings.

We are reminded in this book that we have medicalized death as a problem to solve, rather than recognizing it as an internal experience that will always be with us. We do not solve death any more than we solve life. The quote at beginning of this Foreword reminds us that our grief reactions, whatever they are, remain reasonable once we consider the context.

This is an important book, one of those few which make a human and humane difference in the world. Through sharing the pain, we experience the joy more fully. I am deeply thankful for learning what has come to me through the reading of *Gili's Book*. I am sure you will profit as much as I in your encounter with Henya Kagan (Klein) and her daughter Gili Klein.

Allen E. Ivey, Ed.D., A.B.P.P.
Distinguished University Professor
University of Massachusetts, Amherst

Acknowledgments

I would have written this book even if it was the last thing I ever did in this life, because I promised it to Gili after her death. But Norm (my late husband), Joy and Dr. John Barrand, Rabbi Dr. Jack Segal, Rabbi Betzalel Marinovsky and his wife Lea, Dr. Gay Goodman, Darlene and Lisa Taylor, Becky Smith, Meg Holmes, Lisa Kelly, Christy Rouleau, Dr. Aksel Sarid, Dr. Ellen Gritz, Dr. Lois Friedman, Ronnie Bibliowicz, Michal Inbar, Tal Haran, Amalya Mirvis, Dr. Barbara Paul, Connie Brandt, Shai Ben-Zvi, and, most of all, Alan Levine made the process more bearable. Some listened to my broken heart. Some went to the library for me or edited my chapters. And others gave love, trust, and support, which made my journey less lonely. I am forever grateful to all of them.

The book would not necessarily have been published had it not been for two compassionate people. The first one is Dr. Allen Ivey, who believed in my message. The other is Carol Collins, the editor at Teachers College Press to whom Allen Ivey gave my manuscript. Carol's deep involvement with the manuscript, along with her creative ideas and gentle guidance, taught me yet another lesson of kindness. To them, too—my deepest gratitude.

My Dead

"only the dead don't die."

Only they are left me, they are faithful still
whom death's sharpest knife can no longer kill.

At the turn of the highway, at the close of the day
they silently surround me, they quietly go my way.

A true pact is ours, a tie time cannot dissever.
Only what I have lost is what I possess forever.

Ra'hel, *Flowers of Perhaps*
(R. Friend & S. Sandbank, trans.;
London: Menard Press, 1995)

PRELUDE

"A Love That Has No Boundaries"

Gili, my beautiful 11-year-old daughter, was killed. She died on January 3, 1990, 5 days after a speeding driver drove her car straight into Gili's seat in the back of her stepfather's car. It happened at the entrance to our house, only 30 feet away from where I sat waiting for her with a festive Chanukah dinner.

When Gili died, I felt my life had ended with her because she was my life. (A friend said, "When your child was alive, you projected; when she died, you internalized.") I tried to will myself to die; I even tried to kill myself, but I survived. I felt as though I was doomed to live, and for a long time I just existed, hanging on by a thread.

Then I started listening to Gili's voice in me, urging me to *live*, not just exist. She reminded me that I have a mission to fulfill—mine and hers. I am a helper, I thought. I am a psychologist. Gili had wanted to become a child psychologist. Is the mission—Gili's and mine—to help children? To help parents? To redefine a reason for living, I found out, was the hardest of all. I'm still struggling. I would still rather be with Gili than on this earth.

Ironically, as a psychologist, I had often worked with bereaved parents and children (I wonder now if I truly helped any of the bereaved). Yet I could not be helped when I became a bereaved parent myself. I found out through experience that many in the helping professions do not fully understand parental mourning. I found out that the notion of mourning in stages, phases, or tasks did not reflect my experience, and I doubt that it reflects the mourning of other bereaved parents. Based on my personal experience and professional observation of other bereaved parents, I think that mourning is an "all feelings at once" phenomenon, not one of "feelings in stages."

To this day, I struggle with the term *loss*. Similar to Anne Puryear (1996) in her book, *Stephen Lives!*, I too feel that ". . . no one is ever lost to anyone they love." And "to lose" my child implies that I was not responsible or caring enough to keep her; the term places the responsibility on the parent, and as such it enhances the sense of guilt and shame. But in spite of the pain this term triggers, I will continue using it for its convenience.

1

I *know* that losing one's child to death is different from any other type of loss. I have suffered other losses, too—a father at a young age, close friends, and, recently, my husband, Gili's stepfather. Only 4 years and 4 months after Gili was killed, Norman Kagan, my beloved husband, died after a brief struggle with lung cancer. And there were many other losses— my country and my language when moving to the United States, my job, my friends and family after Gili's death and after Norm's death. However, the experience of losing Gili was the most devastating of all and different from the other losses on many levels—emotionally, cognitively, physiologi- cally, and spiritually. I began to ask myself whether I was supposed to share my new understanding with other bereaved parents and children. Was I supposed to write a book? Was this to become part of my mission? Many books have been written about "how to mourn well and how to go on with your life." I was not comforted by these books, nor was I enlight- ened. Although I found a phrase here and there, a word or an idea that helped to crystallize my thinking and feeling, nevertheless, as a whole, I felt I was not helped. I therefore decided to write my own book. I had to write a book that not only describes my reactions to this horrendous loss but also tells who Gili was—what kind of a person she was—so the reader better understands the magnitude of my loss. I felt a need to continue my dialogue with Gili, who was, as she said, my best friend "in the whole wide world."

This book is a wake-up call. It is what mourners as well as those work- ing with the bereaved need to hear. It is not about how to mourn well and how to go on with your life. Instead it is a trip straight into the depths of horror—an intense examination of a mother mourning the sudden death of her daughter. I am not going to stroke you and tell you that the pain will ever go away, that life will be wonderful one day. Rather, I hope to grab you by the shoulders and shake you and tell you: "The pain is here to stay! The depth to which you love is the depth to which you will hurt. You cannot run away from the pain, nor should you. Also, you are alone in your pain and in your grieving, as you are in your search for the meaning in what happened." Ironically, I find this realization to be comforting—it acknowledges the reality of the bereaved. You cannot expect that anyone else, not even those closest to you, will feel the same way you feel and experience the loss. You had a unique relationship with your child, with your sibling, or with your husband. Your mourning, then, is a reflection of that relationship and of many other factors that played a role in your life. Your mourning is unique, as your life and relationships are; therefore you cannot expect to have companionship in your mourning. Not all of us search for meaning, but even if you only ask, "Why?!" your "why" will be differ- ent from someone else's. It is my conviction that the sooner you accept that reality, although you may not agree with it, the better equipped you will become to cope with your new life's challenges.

Although this book is mainly for you, the bereaved parent and the professional who works with grieving parents, it is also a memorial for Gili—for the kind of person she was, for her dream to help children, and for our love for each other, which has no boundaries of time and of physical existence. My intention in commemorating Gili's life is to send a message to our society. Society reveals its values about children not only by protective laws but also by whom it commemorates. There are memorials for adults who have died. How common is it to find a memorial for a child, or a biography of a child who lived and deeply affected our lives and still continues to have a profound and lasting effect on us? Was creating such a memorial to become another part of my mission?

Gili's answer to me was "yes." I have chosen to do this through the format of a dialogue with Gili. Some of the dialogue really took place when she was alive, and some of it I could hear, see, or feel only in my mind. Through the dialogue, I hope that you will get to know Gili as a real person. I want you to be able to hear her voice, to see her in your mind's eye, and to feel her spirit. But most importantly, I want you to feel the magnitude of my grief and the totality of my loss, in order to better know your own loss. I want you to cry for Gili with me, and as you cry, you will cry for your own child, and for yourself. I want us to scream together, "Why?!" Maybe the skies will open up! I also want to tell you that being one of the "walking dead" is sometimes the only way we, the bereaved, can be, and it's normal and OK. Don't measure your "progress" according to someone else's timetable or theoretical stages. Listen to your pain, and let it tell you how and what to do or not to do. Let your child's voice come through. Listen to this voice and let it guide you.

I feel that my mission will be complete if I can reach out to you from the bottom of my despair and touch you in your grief. My hope is that you, too, will be able to lessen your sense of being alone by touching someone else—perhaps a grieving child. I hope that together we will find a way for our children to stay alive in our hearts and for us, the survivors, to live, not just to exist. Reaching out to others and *living*—not just existing—are crucial.

THE ORGANIZATION OF THE BOOK

The first part of this book, *Beginning and End: Gili's Life*, is a dialogue with Gili, while looking together at her album pictures, that tells the story of her life and death. The story began in Israel, where Gili was born, and ended prematurely in Houston, Texas. Gili's voice comes across in the dialogue, her artwork, and her writings. A foundation is thus laid to understand the depth of my loss, and of society's as well. I consider the first part (Chapters 1 to 4) to be the soul of the book. I changed the names of people, except for Gili and Norm, and of certain places.

In the Interlude, I describe my initial reactions to Gili's sudden death and premonitions that, in retrospect, it appears that both she and I had. This account marks the beginning of my venture into a spiritual quest. *End and Beginning: Life Without Gili* is the second half of the book. In it, from Chapters 5 through 8, I describe my search for an answer to the unanswerable question: "Why?" I describe why and how I developed a new concept of parental bereavement, defining concepts of living and surviving, hope and mission, and what "readjustment" means in this context. In the process of my search, I discovered that current theoretical models of bereavement do not apply to my situation. The attempt to develop a general model of grieving that can be applied to every type of bereavement may be a misguided endeavor. Metaphorically speaking, from a general description of humanity we can learn little or nothing about one individual, but from a specific description of one individual, we can learn an enormous amount about humanity. Therefore I decided to present a model of bereavement that applies mainly to bereaved parents, especially to parents whose children died a sudden death. Some principles of this model can be applied to similar types of bereavement, and in that way, as well as in its usefulness to other bereaved parents, I hope my experience can transcend the boundaries of my personal tragedy. I have named this new concept *the readjustment model of parental bereavement*, because I perceive parents' survival after the death of their child as a dynamic process of relearning patterns of feeling, thinking, and acting; it is a lifelong process of readjusting to live with mourning, since there is no "recovery" or "healing" from the death of one's child.

In Chapter 8, I describe *deep sadness*, a term I coined, as a specific type of grief, typical to parental grieving, that is distinguished from depression. There is a tendency for counselors and clients alike to confuse the two, to mask the grief reactions of clients, and inhibit their expression, by the use of medication. This is especially true when the bereaved parent did not suffer from any mood or anxiety disorders prior to the death of the child. *It is important that the bereaved parents cope with their grief by experiencing the pain to its full intensity.* I argue against the attempt to pathologize parental bereavement, a trend especially evident in the literature affected by the medical way of thinking. A careful analysis of the parents' histories, lifestyles, values, and beliefs, to mention a few factors, will provide valuable information to assist professionals in their assessment of the effects of bereavement. I discuss the concepts of living versus surviving and of hope and mission. I conclude that a turning point in parental bereavement occurs when the parents identify a mission to live for.

If Chapters 1 to 4 are the soul of the book, then Chapter 8 is the heart. In this chapter I describe the dynamics of the process of parental bereavement. First, I define the concept of readjustment and describe its characteristics and progress. Second, I explain what simultaneous inward and outward steps mean and how balance is maintained. Then, I take a closer look at specific intense emotions, particularly anger: Usually considered by professionals to be destructive to the grieving parent, anger can be productive and necessary to the process of grief. I discuss how to recognize readjustment and end the chapter with suggestions for mental health professionals regarding factors to consider in treating bereaved parents.

In the Postlude, I reflect on the path I have taken so far and consider what is still awaiting me and other bereaved parents.

PART I

Beginning and End: Gili's Life

CHAPTER 1

First Discoveries: Ashkelon, Israel (August 25, 1978–August 1981)

Come, Tooki, let us look at your album pictures, and I will tell the story of your life. I never told you these stories before, so come.

"And my death?"

Yes, that too, but later, Giligooli. Snuggle up to my heart's side now. Let me put my arm around you and squeeze you closer to me. Although I can see and feel you solid in my arms only in my sleep, I sense your presence now.

"Mommy, am I a ghost now?"

I guess you might say so. But you are my sweet ghost, not some scary one. I can tell that it amuses you. You'd like to sneak up on me and yell "Boo!" wouldn't you? You laugh; I caught you.

You always asked me to look at pictures with you and to tell you the stories behind each one of them. You loved to do that with friends who came to visit you, too. But I rarely made the time for that. There were always things to do that seemed to be more important than looking at albums. Because of my recent marriage and my newfound happiness, I gradually developed the notion that you and I would always have a "tomorrow." How little did I know! Now I have time. I am finally available to you, now that I have resigned all of my professional responsibilities, now that Norm, your stepfather, has died, too. I can listen to you, my love. I can look at your albums—the albums that I finally made after you were killed.

I sit and look at your pictures and scream to God; sometimes I scream in silence, and sometimes aloud. "Gotteniu in Himmel! Why?! Please, let me see and hear my child one more time! Let me feel her in my arms just once!"

So here you are in my arms.

You were just a few days old and were looking at me in serious concentration, with wide-open eyes. To me, this funny-looking picture symbolizes the continuation of our bond, which started when you were still growing under my heart, and into it.

Gili, only a few days old

I named you *Gili* before you were born. It's written in the Kabbalah, the mystical interpretation of the Torah (the first five books of the Bible), that the soul is directed by God to choose her name before she is born, and the parents are then directed to give this name to the newborn. If so, my love, you could not have chosen a better name for yourself. *Gili* means "be joyful" and "my joy" in Hebrew. You lived up to your name, as though there were a mission in it. You felt that it was your responsibility to make the people you cared about happy, or at least to feel good about themselves. I especially remember a few incidents where I was amazed at your maturity and kindness. Whenever I cried, you would rush and bring me a glass of water, urging me to drink it. "Drink, Ima [Mommy], it will make you feel better," you would say to me in a soft voice and with a smile. Then you would touch my hand or face in a feather-like touch. God, how much I miss that touch! I think that you believed that the water you gave me had magical healing powers, just like my kiss when you were hurting.

"Mommy, I want you to feel joy again. I am happy now. I feel free and I still live up to my name!"

I am beginning to feel joy occasionally, and I am relieved to know that you are happy, my love; but even so, how can I be "happy"? You are still beyond my reach, and I am still "stuck" here.

On another occasion, when you had just started middle school, you noticed a classmate sitting alone in the hallway at school. You walked over to her, introduced yourself, and asked her how she felt. Then you made a habit of talking to that girl every day.

"How do you know?"

That girl told us about it in a letter she wrote to us when she found out that you had been killed. She said that she usually felt very lonely and unwanted by the other children. You always had a kind word for her, and you made her feel special. The girl added that she misses "seeing you walking down the hallway with your shiny hair and bright smile." One of your teachers at Purple Owls Middle School told an acquaintance of ours that "in my middle-age cynical life, a child like Gili made me believe in God again." Hannah, your stepgrandmother, said to me many times, "I met Gili only once, but I was so impressed with her. She was such a kind and understanding child. She was so careful not to hurt anybody's feelings." When I asked Hannah what she was referring to, she told me that, on our wedding day, she saw you giving a flower to a young woman. When you noticed that Hannah was looking at you, you walked over to her and gently handed her a flower, too. Hannah said, "She touched my heart deeply."

"Mommy, it's embarrassing; don't make me into an angel."

I'm sorry, but it is all true. Although there were a few times when I was abrupt with you or even angry, it was not because you had done anything that deserved a scolding but because I was in one of my impatient moods. But one glorious smile from you or a gentle apology (when you were the one who deserved *my* apology) made me feel ashamed that I had hurt you. How many times I have replayed these painful moments in my mind, and wished every time that a lightning bolt would have struck me then—or at least that I could have erased your hurt.

"Ima, but you used to apologize to me when you thought that you hurt me. And I knew that you sounded angrier than you really were."

Thank you for saying that. Sometimes I feel so much shame and so much guilt that I wish to die. You see? I make no attempt to idealize you. I know that neither of us was perfect, but you were definitely very close to that. And besides, what's wrong with emphasizing the good? You were my angel. You still are. L. M. Montgomery, one of your favorite authors, described her heroine in the *Chronicles of Avonlea* in these words, "She had a way of embroidering life with stars." This was exactly how I always saw you, my love. Remember? I used to tell you that you were the best person that I had ever known. I used to tell you that you were beautiful, inside as well as outside. You were always embarrassed hearing me say that. I suspected that it pleased you, too, although you were too modest to admit it. Did it?

"Yes, Mommy. I loved that and the nicknames that you gave me, like Tooki and Giligooli."

"I love my name" you used to say. "It's short and special."

You liked Klein, your last name, too. You giggled when my mother, "Savta Aimi," used to affectionately call you "klein Gili" ("little Gili" in Yiddish). When you were 10 years old, and Norm and I got married, for a while you experimented by incorporating a "K" as your middle initial. It gave you a feeling of belonging. I add your last name to mine now.

"Why in parentheses?"

I write it in parentheses because the symbol looks to me as if it hugs your name—as if you're hugged, to emphasize our bond.

"I like that."

When you were still a baby, your father and I used to jokingly wonder whether in your old age you would change your name to a more serious, adult-like name. Whoever heard of a "Grandma Gili," we'd laugh. Well, we don't need to worry about that anymore. Yes, Gili, I know how you would have responded to my last comment. You could always sense my pain. I can visualize you now, tilting your head so gently to your left shoulder and looking at me with teary eyes. You would understand and know the depth of my daily horror of living without you. You would feel deep sorrow for not being able to help me now in any visible way.

"Mommy, I understand you truly. But I don't want you to hurt so. I want you to live, not just to exist. And as part of your mission, Mommy, I want you to tell our story—yours and mine, not just my story only—as you promised me after I died."

Yes, my love, but do you understand that this is exactly the essence of my struggle—I don't want to live without you. If I have to, I'd rather exist until it's my time to join you. I would like to be able to promise you that I'll learn to live and fulfill our missions. I am not sure that I can promise you that—not yet. I see you looking at me with your wise and knowing look, as though you know something that I don't know yet. Now I feel a smile starting to climb up your little face, right into your big blue eyes. Your eyes seem to shine from inside. You are smiling, Tooki sheli. Your long dark eyelashes cast a gentle shadow on your smooth cheeks.

"Not an equal shadow!"

Yes, not an equal shadow. I remember. Only a few months before the accident, you experimented by cutting off the eyelashes of only one eye!

Was it your right eye? You told me that you were curious. You asked your-self, "What will I look like with no eyelashes, or with short ones?"

For a while, it made me wonder what to expect from you as a "soon-to-be teenager." You "softened" the surprise by leaving a funny, though ac-curate, drawing of your eyes—one with normal eyelashes and the other with drastically shortened eyelashes. Then, we laughed. Now, I look at your drawing, and I cry.

Some say that the soul is reflected in the eyes. I say, your soul was re-flected both in your eyes and in your smile. You had many other beautiful features, too. Your most memorable feature was your warm smile. You had a beautiful, open smile that started in your heart, climbed to your huge, soulful blue-gray eyes, and spread to your rosebud lips. Your eyebrows were silky brown, and they arched over your big blue eyes. The slightly downward angle of your eyes sometimes gave you a hint of a sad expres-sion. You had a small oval face and very soft, pale golden skin. Your small straight nose was the genetic contribution of my side of the family, and your big toes, which I loved, were from your father's side.

Gili before and after cutting off the
eyelashes of her right eye

You wore glasses from the time you were 3 years old. Because your skin was so delicate, I was concerned that your glasses would leave a permanent mark on the bridge of your nose. In fact, a slight pressure mark did start to show up. I suggested contact lenses, but you refused for a long time, saying, "I love my glasses." Then one day late in November of 1989, a short time before the accident, you came home from school, floating, not walking. You had a big smile on your face, and you told me that one of the nicer boys in class had told you that with your glasses you looked like a nerd but without your glasses you looked neat. He told you, "Gili, you really have beautiful eyes." You were flattered by that comment, and I laughed with joy. Was it your first "serious" compliment from a boy? You told me then that you would "like to think about contact lenses right after Christmas break." For an instant, I could envision you as a young woman, glowing with first love. Your chance for first love never came, my child.

You had a long delicate neck, and your hair was incredibly full and silky from the time you were a baby. It shone like dim gold or dark wheat. Although you once described your hair color as "dirty blond," I didn't like that description. At the time of your death (*your death*!), your hair was cut in a pageboy haircut. God! Where were you when Gili needed you, when we all needed you?! You told me, "I like my hair a little bit longer," and you pointed to shoulder length. You liked to wear your hair away from your face, pulled back by a bow or pins. You left some bangs on your forehead. For a while, I wore your bow and let my hair grow to shoulder length. This was another way to feel "one" with you.

You had pierced ears. For your second birthday, Rivka, your babysitter, surprised us by taking you to somebody (we never figured out to whom) to pierce your ears. She then put little golden earrings, shaped like stars, in your ears. It took me some time to get used to the idea that my baby was not whole anymore, that there were two little holes in your tiny earlobes. It bothered me because I was afraid that children would ridicule you, as they had ridiculed me when I was a young child. Pierced ears and golden earrings, at that time in Israel, were almost a giveaway that one was an immigrant or newcomer. I was an immigrant, but you, my baby, were a proud "sabra" (a native Israeli). It turned out that you grew up in the United States and not in Israel, so the pierced ears became another reason for you to be happy. You could wear any type of earrings. You liked to wear earrings, mostly the ones that you designed and made. And typically, your entire appearance was always neat and understated.

"I remember, sometimes I would say to you, Mommy, I know that you would like me to wear more fashionable or flashier clothes, but I like it this way, and I hope that you are not disappointed."

Of course, I was disappointed sometimes, but I had tremendous respect for your opinions and the choices you made. I hope that I never failed to tell you so.

From a chubby baby, you grew up to be a tall, slim, long-legged girl. At the time of your death, you were already about 5'2", almost my height, and you weighed about 75 pounds. I still cannot associate *death* with you, my child. Your hands were very expressive, and you had long, strong fingers and slightly squarish fingernails. You tried to grow them "just a little bit" so your hands would "look prettier," more adult-like. "Middle school made me feel very grown up. Mommy, don't forget my rings and the bump on my middle finger on my right hand."

How can I? Every time I look at my own "bump," I remember yours. The writer's corn, as I referred to it, was another genetic bond between you and me.

I loved your distinctive knuckles, which made your hands look artistic; and you were very artistic. I used to refer to your hands as wise and smart. They were constantly busy doing something, as though they had a life of their own. When you were excited, you used to "talk" with your hands. I do that, too.

You giggle, "Ima, I'm sure that without our hands we would have been mute."

On your left hand, you wore the ring I gave you—a golden band with a tiny, light-colored opal. Your father had given it to me when I received my doctorate. Later, I wanted you to have it. On your right hand, you wore a thin silver ring with two little dangling hearts. Doris, your best friend, gave it to you. Both rings were damaged by the medical staff, who tried to remove them on the day of the accident. You also wore a bead bracelet that you had made of Fimo, a clay-like material that you used to make miniature sculptures and other decorative items from, baking them in the oven to harden them. I put it all together in your last album, one of the albums that you will never see!

"But I do, Ima. I really do in ways that I cannot explain."

You had a soft voice—sweet and melodic. When you were excited, you would make brief pauses that sounded like "em . . . em . . ." and finish your sentences with a question mark. To emphasize what you were saying, you used to raise your right index finger and shake it in excitement. You used to pronounce your S's with the tip of your tongue, between your front teeth. We loved it, because it made you forever sound a little bit "babyish," but your second-grade teacher in Carbondale, Illinois, didn't.

"She sent me for a whole semester to Mrs. Buzscowsky, the speech therapist." You remember. For children who have difficulties with certain speech sounds, this teacher's name was a nightmare. It gave us many laughs. You used to take a deep breath before pronouncing her name, and you used to beg us not to ask you to repeat her name! Mrs. Buzscowsky was surprised that you would say your S's correctly in class but during break, when talking to the other children, you pronounced the S in your typical way. When I asked you about it, you responded, "Why can't she understand? I can say S correctly when I want to, but I like to say it my way!" Then one day you came home from school and, smiling from ear to ear, excitedly exclaimed, "Mrs. Buzscowsky!" We knew then that you had successfully graduated. We assumed the final test was to pronounce the teacher's name correctly. We all collapsed laughing.

You had many funny gestures. Do you remember how you used to "wiggle your tail," mimicking Shelly, your puppy, when you were happy? I would then embrace you very tightly, as if I was trying to squeeze you into my heart; this funny, loving gesture of yours moved me so deeply.

You were loved! On your headstone we had engraved, "A child more loved never walked on earth." You were conceived in love and you were born into love.

Do you remember the story I told you about my attempt to raise you as a vegetarian?

"The story about you and daddy 'milking' almonds for me at 4:00 in the morning, so I wouldn't have to drink cow milk and get belly cramps?"

You are laughing. It was not funny then—after an hour of boiling, peeling, and squeezing the almonds to death, we finally had half a cup of milk for you. With shaky hands I poured it into a bottle and very carefully brought it to your pouting lips. We watched you very intently. You took only one sip—and then you let out a scream that awakened the neighbors. But not before you spat the stuff out with the most disgusted expression I have ever seen on a baby's face—you were only 4 months old and already knew what you didn't like. We laughed so hard that day, but we never tried it again. Loving you was easy! I have never known anybody who possessed a greater ability to love and to express love than you did. I went through your belongings after you died, and I found a letter you had written to a friend describing our hugs in these words, "My mom and I squeeze our hearts out of each other."

You loved your father and your brother, Guy, very much, and they loved you as much, but you and I were mother and daughter, twin souls.

"Soulmates!"

Even better. We were mother and daughter, best friends. I always loved you more than I loved my life. And I still do. You loved me as nobody else ever did. I feel you still do.

"I do!"

You keep touching me in so many profound ways. Your legacy motivates me to search for meaning and mission for my life—your visitations reinforce my belief that love and life are eternal, and they instill hope in me, for we will be together again. I can only hope that my heart touches you where my hands cannot, because I lack words to describe how much I miss you!

"I wish I could reassure you, Ima, that I can hear, see, and feel you. And that I come to visit you often. I wish that knowing that would comfort you."

It does, sometimes. And other times I am skeptical and doubtful about all of it.

*   *   *

Thus far I have described you. I want everyone to be able to visualize you, the heroine of this story. I want them to know who you were and some of what happened to you. Now I would like to go back to your early days in Israel. Let's go back to Ashkelon, to the days of my pregnancy. I was so happy to be pregnant with you. However, there were some issues that clouded my happiness. For one thing, Guy had already experienced suffering: emotional and physical. In addition, from my earliest memories I had a premonition that an ultimate tragedy was awaiting me.

"Why, Mommy?"

I am not sure that I can really explain. How can I explain an intuitive feeling? When you were born, I had a sinking feeling that persisted, and it became more specific as you grew up. I became terrified of losing you. When your brother was ill, I was afraid of losing him, too, but it was different. It was not because I loved him less than you. You seemed more fragile than he. I believe that my fears stemmed from my premonition.

"That's scary, Ima. You never told me."

How could I? I didn't know what it meant and whether to believe it or not.

"Do you still have a premonition?"

No, my love, I don't. The ultimate horror has already happened.

Despite my premonition, I was elated when you were born. I had the illusion that we would be happy and live forever. You were born on August 25, 1978 (Virgo), at 2:45 in the morning, and your father was at my side. Guy was almost 9 years old then. He wanted to have a baby brother, but he happily welcomed a baby sister.

Your father said, "She came out from you like a drawer." You were the most beautiful baby in the neighborhood, or so the neighbors said. Of course, in my eyes, you were the most beautiful baby in the "whole wide world" (your favorite expression). You were born into a protective, loving family, or so I wanted to believe. However, this "loving" family fell apart when your father and I got a divorce. Guy "divorced" us then, too. It hurt badly. You and I cried a lot because of that, but you never failed to tell me,

"Mommy, don't cry. He will come back to us, one day." You were right! He came back when Norm died. He is my friend now. My mother and sister were supportive after my divorce from your father, from a distance. But when you were killed, my protective and loving family disintegrated. This time, they chose to eliminate both of us (and Norm) from their lives. I expected our family to love us, to be protective, caring, and compassionate. But my perception of my family was only a myth. So here we are, alone. I know, you keep reminding me, "And Guy, don't forget my Guy."

I don't, Yalda sheli, I don't.

I do a lot of remembering these days. As I think back to your early days in Ashkelon, I remember how we used to walk around the neighborhood—you in your stroller, with me pushing you. I put a red, bow-shaped pin in your hair, so people immediately would know that you were a girl! (Remember how you were hurt 9 years later when you got a haircut and somebody asked me, "What's your son's name?" We both were ready to kill that woman!)

Although Guy was often in the hospital, when he was home, he would take you for a short walk in the stroller. He didn't mind playing with you as long as it was inside the house. I suspect that he even enjoyed it, but he didn't do it too often. I guess that he was embarrassed for his classmates to see him with his baby sister—you were a girl after all. I can hear you saying with an all-knowing smile, "Yes, Ima, boys are weird."

We lived in a small, white-painted house in Afridar. It was a typical middle-class neighborhood in Ashkelon, the Biblical Delilah's hometown. Our house was surrounded by a big lawn, trees, and flowers. The most prominent tree in our yard was an acacia tree probably more than 100 years old. That tree was struck by lightning years later when our lives started falling apart: How symbolic!

From the windows of your room, we could see, hear, and even smell the beautiful blue Mediterranean Sea. Very often, you and I would go to the beach. Gili, remember how the Mediterranean sunlight leaves very sharp shadows? It makes everything look distinct and very well defined. That might be one of the reasons why you and I always had a need to define or to describe things very clearly.

I remember kneeling beside you. Looking at the sky and the water from the height of your eyes made me feel as though we were both floating in an infinite ocean of blue. In the days to come, blue became your favorite color; mine, too.

Until your seventh year, you had an unexpectedly low voice for a child, especially for one who looked as gentle and fragile as you did.

"When did it change?"

I don't remember the exact time, but when you were about 9 years old, your voice became very melodic, soft and sweet. You always had a rich singing voice, and you loved to sing. Your voice is etched on my mind. I really don't need a tape recording to remind me of your talking, whispering, or singing. But I wish that I had used a tape recorder, on one particular day. A couple of days before the accident, you were singing in your bathroom. I was drawn upstairs by the sound of your singing. It was the first time I ever heard you singing like that. Your voice was magical. It was mature, with an adult-like quality. It was moving smoothly between octaves. Although powerful, it had no sharp edges. Your voice had a velvety quality. I was glued to your bathroom door. I stood there awestruck that this voice was coming out of you, and you were only 11 years old. I was overcome with emotions. When you came out of the bathroom, I asked you whether you would like to take singing lessons. You responded shyly, "No, Mommy, I just like to sing to myself."

I do have a tape recording of you singing when you were almost 3 years old. I remember one time you were standing on our bed and pretending to sing into a microphone—"Lu hayiti yeled" (If I was only a child), a popular song in the Israeli Children's Song Festival that year. You amazed us with your accurate memory of words and melody.

"Mommy, the singing-in-the-bathroom story reminded me of another 'bathroom experience.' Remember how I used to lock myself in my bathroom whenever I got upset with you or with Norm?"

Yeah, you used to "talk out-loud" your misery.

"My bathroom was my refuge!"

Aha. And what always amazed Norm and me was how you came out of that bathroom.

"Running toward the two of you, but especially to you, Mommy, with open arms, asking you to give me a hug."

Norm and I used to shake our heads in amazement; neither of us had ever known anybody like you. My heart expanded with love and admiration looking at you. You were growing up to be such a fine person. You already showed so much maturity and integrity.

As I continue going through your albums, I am reminded how much you loved stuffed animals—better than dolls. You loved to walk around with a "baby" animal, pretending that you were the "Mommy." Until your last day, every night before bedtime you used to select from 10 to 20 stuffed animals to sleep with you. Every animal had a name, and every animal had a special reason to sleep with you that night. For instance, Benji, your tiny dog with the crossed sad eyes, had a constant case of "missing Mommy" and had to sleep with you. Now I take him with me when I'm out of town. You also used to sleep with Doobi, the white teddy bear that Norm gave me. You told me that you wanted part of me with you at night. When I'm alone now, Doobi sleeps in my arms because I want part of you with me at night, too. The nurturing characteristic showed up in you many times in your life—in your love and your caring about animals, small children, children your age, and, of course, us. Because of your nurturing character, I used to call you *Mommile* ("little mother" in Yiddish). Even at the young age of less than 3, you showed an incredible ability to express love. You were very affectionate with us, with children you loved, and with other people you knew, but very shy with people you didn't know. However, your shyness did not keep you closed. You were observant of others and wanted to reach out, but you were aware of your shyness. I remember that once on the beach in Galveston, you wanted to go over to a girl about your age who was playing by herself, but you were too shy to do so. You asked me then, "Mommy, what should I do?" I answered with a question, "What would you like to do?"

You said to me, "I would like to introduce myself to her. Then I would ask her what her name is and if she would like to play with me." After "rehearsing" that, you walked over to the girl, and, although I could not hear you, I could see you talking. I learned another lesson from you—how to overcome my shyness. But I don't have you to "rehearse" with me.

"Ima, tell me about the pacifier, please."

OK, I see that you like this picture. You got attached to a pacifier right from the beginning—my idea and, according to others, my mistake. I thought it would help you with your teething. I did not anticipate a "pacifier addiction." Your pacifier and you were inseparable. You showed strong loyalty to one particular pacifier—the more ragged it became, the more you liked it. If you could have written poetry at the time, you would have described its exact gooey texture, its special smell that helped you recognize it in the dark, and its adorable fading colors of brown and yellow.

"Gold!"

I won't argue with you. Only "pacifier lovers" understand the difference. I accepted the pacifier as an integral part of your body, in spite of grandma's and neighbors' "good" advice. You finally gave it up when you where 5 years old. You did it on the plane, on our way back from your first visit to Israel. When we arrived home, you and I built a little house with a comfortable bed for it. With shaky hands, you put the worn-out, battered pacifier in its new home. Then you placed the little house right next to your pillow saying, "Just in case it will feel lonely and I'll have to put it in my mouth." You gave it a final kiss and said to it a last "Laila tov" (good night). That was it until just a few days before December 29, 1989, the day of the accident.

You and I were in a drug store when you shyly told me that you would like to feel a pacifier in your mouth, "one more time" because you missed its taste. Your "confession" touched me deeply. It sounded so final. You looked so fragile and were so vulnerable. Without any questions, I bought

Gili as a toddler with her pacifier

the tiny pink pacifier that you selected while you were looking around, hoping that nobody would see you. You looked at me tenderly, grateful that I respected you enough not to ask, "Why?" I knew why. At that time, you were very anxious about your father's upcoming visit. You begged him time and again, "Please don't come now. I need time to adjust to my new life. I love you, Daddy, but please let me breathe now. I'll come to visit you in Israel in the summer if you promise to let me go back home, to Ima." At the store, your eyes slowly filled with tears, and I was choked up. With gentle tenderness, we embraced each other for a long moment. Then you asked me not to tell anybody, and I promised. Forgive me now for break- ing my promise. When we came home, after you tried it once, you put the pacifier in your drawer. "It doesn't taste as good as I remember it. It's not soft, and it smells different," you said in disillusionment, realizing that the pacifier was not the security blanket you needed. It was still in your drawer, where you left it until I moved to my new house. Sometimes I was tempted to touch it with my lips and pretend to feel your lips there. You were right, Yalda sheli, it was not soft, and it felt different.

When you were about 1 year old , I noticed that whenever you tried to focus on something, you squinted with your right eye. I knew that some- thing was wrong when you began calling any child that you saw from a distance by your brother's name. Since your father and I are nearsighted, I suspected that you might be, too. Your eyesight was checked, but the specialist could not determine whether you were nearsighted. An accurate diagnosis was made in the United States when you were 3 years old. You were diagnosed as having a "lazy eye," and for the rest of your life you wore glasses. To our surprise, you loved your glasses. When you were 10 years old and I asked you the reason, you said, still in wonderment, "I can see, and there is so much to see!" In order to save the affected eye, every day a patch was put on your left eye, the "good" one. Although it went on for months, you never, not once, complained about the discomfort of putting on or removing the patch. You would come to me in the morning, lift your tiny face to me, and ask me to put the patch on. We would say together, "Good night, eye"—you with a little smile of resignation. My brave little baby! You were such a small bundle of sweetness!

I know that I keep jumping back and forth, but it's hard to stop the stream of memories. You know that I was always a storyteller. So let's go back to Ashkelon, Israel, when you were 2 years old.

Making and keeping good friends became one of your characteristics. Your best friends in Afridar, Ashkelon, were two sisters, Sharon and Elena. Sharon was the oldest, and Elena was a year older then you were. On our lawn, you spent many happy hours together sitting in the sun.

"I don't remember it, Ima."

Don't feel sorry. You were only 2 years old, and I noticed that all your memories from the first 3 years of your life in Israel evaporated. This is one of the reasons why I am telling you the story of your life.

Another characteristic of yours was your love for school. Lea, your first teacher, probably set the tone for the years to come. You loved her, and she loved you. Lea used to carry you around in her arms, but even the most loving teacher gets tired sometimes. So one morning, when I took you to kindercare, you lifted your little arms in anticipation of being picked up by Lea as usual. You were surprised to hear her saying, "Not today, Gili. You look very delicate, but you really are heavy!" You did not cry or protest. You looked more puzzled than disappointed. However, from that day on, you discovered that the other children used their legs to get around, not Lea's arms.

Did you know that Lea's daughter died, too? How sad that I can truly feel for her only now. No wonder that we parents feel so alone in our grief. Only those whose beloved children have died can feel for us.

Even at your young age, you showed an exceptional talent for colors and forms, and the minute you held a crayon and paper in your hands, you started drawing. You continued drawing, painting, and sculpting every day of your life. You loved to experiment with various materials and to explore new tastes, new places, and different people. You always were very curious and a very fast learner.

I used to watch you in amazement—the way you touched everything lightly with the tips of your fingers, like a butterfly. It was as if you wanted to reassure yourself of their being and, at the same time, to state your belonging. When I watched you, I used to think that this gesture best expressed the meaning of being part of the Universe and of the spiritual bond that you had and felt with Creation.

Another typical picture of you is etched in my mind. You, on the beach in Ashkelon, holding a delicate straw, trying to trace the fresh footprints that a lady bug was making in front of us. You were sensitive to the size and fragility of the bug. Although you were nearsighted, you searched for just the right straw—one that wouldn't hurt the ladybug if you touched it by accident when tracing its footprints. You loved the beach and exploring the dunes, the flowers, the butterflies, and the bugs. One day on the beach, your father and I were convinced that you would become a biologist. You surprised me a few years later, at age 10, when you declared that human nature was what interested you most and therefore you wanted to become a psychologist, like your parents and your stepfather, Norm. You were very specific about your career plans. You said that you wanted to become "a professor and specialize in child psychology." You dreamed of having a clinic with me. You said with a bright smile, "Mother and daughter psychologists."

When I asked you, "And what about your dream to become an artist and a teacher of art for children?"

You answered in a soft but unusually self-assured voice, "I am an artist; I cannot help it, but I have a lot to learn about people. I want to help children, and as a psychologist I can do that best." I looked at you with so much respect and love. For me, these were moments of self-doubt. I was not sure that I would be capable of continuing to measure up to you as you grew older.

Just before your third birthday, Guy had recovered from his medical condition and we were assured by his doctors that he could travel. Your father and I felt that it was time for us to move on to new horizons, to fulfill old dreams and to provide you and Guy with new opportunities and challenges in America. We celebrated your third birthday in July and promised you another birthday party in America on your real birthday. You were thrilled to receive gifts twice. On August 3, 1981, we left Israel. Books, toys, clothes, and pictures were all packed in eight suitcases. We landed in O'Hare Airport in Chicago 2 days later. This was our first time in America. Our hearts were full of high hopes for the future: hopes for happiness, for success, and for a speedy return to Israel, our real home. But God had different plans for each of us, and especially for you, my love.

CHAPTER 2

A New Path in America: Illinois (August 1981–July 1986)

The night of August 5, 1981, was our first in America. An acquaintance of your father's family met us at O'Hare Airport and took us to the Holiday Inn in downtown Chicago. We arrived at the hotel in the evening, excited but exhausted and hungry. Who could eat with butterflies in our stomachs! We got a room on the 27th floor. We had never been in a skyscraper before. Your father and brother roamed around the room getting ready to go to bed. You and I walked over to the huge window and just stood there for a long time. We hugged each other and trembled with excitement and fatigue. I was flooded by ambivalent emotions—joy and hope, fear and insecurity.

Pointing to the view, you exclaimed many times that evening, "Ima, Ima, tireei, tireei!" ("Mother, Mother, look, look!"). We were transfixed by the incredible view of Chicago bathed in lights. It looked as though America was winking at us with millions of stars. I saw it as a good omen. Little did I know! Finally, we went to bed—you in my arms in one bed, and "the boys" in a separate bed. I tried to engulf you with the shreds of the security that I felt at that moment. I watched all of my family slowly drifting off to sleep. You were sucking your pacifier in a peaceful rhythm while hugging your favorite stuffed animal. You looked so small and fragile, lying in a big foreign bed. I felt so lost. I finally fell into a dreamless sleep.

On our first morning in our new home, we got a real "welcome to America." We left the hotel in two taxies in order to accommodate all of our luggage (filled with most of the material things we had on earth). We headed toward the train station, from which we would leave for our destination, Urbana–Champaign. We arrived and had almost completed unloading when one of the taxi drivers took off with one of our suitcases, disappearing instantly. After the immediate shock I said to myself, "Welcome to America. I want to go home." Sometimes, I cannot avoid wondering whether you, my child, would still be alive if we had done exactly that—gone back home. Because of the turmoil, we missed the train. We arrived in Urbana–Champaign that afternoon in a rented car. Your father joked that the theft of the suitcase worked out fine because there was no room in the car for more luggage. This was the first time we had laughed since we had arrived in America.

The road to Urbana was long and tiring. At one point you asked, "Kvar higanu le Ashkelon?" ("Have we arrived in Ashkelon already?") This was the second time that day that we howled in laughter. "Urbana!" we corrected you. We tried to imprint the new word in your mind. "Urbana," you mumbled in a sleepy voice, pronouncing it with a throaty "r" like an Israeli. Only three weeks later you were pronouncing it like a native.

After 3 hours of driving we arrived at a motel in Urbana, where we would stay for a week until our apartment in University of Illinois student housing was ready. We settled down into one room with two twin beds—one for the "boys" and one for the "girls." It was hot and humid, worse than Israel in August, but weather typical of central Illinois. Guy jumped into the pool immediately. You and I just watched him. At that time you didn't swim yet; only a few years later you became as excellent a swimmer as Guy. To our amazement, we heard Guy chatting in English with a young man while swimming in the pool. We were deeply impressed with his linguistic talent and courage. With a concerned look on your face, you asked me if I thought that you'd ever speak English. I kissed your serious little face, and promised you that you would not only speak English but that you would also dream in English. Your face lit up in a glorious smile of relief and amusement; you liked the idea of dreaming in English.

The first night in Urbana found us lying in one bed hugging each other, trying to digest the events since we had arrived in the States. We needed the reassurance and comfort of our togetherness. We cried and laughed and lulled each other to sleep, secure in each others' arms. Looking back, that night in the motel was the last night that the four of us were ever again really together—united, pulsating with one heart. Even around your deathbed my love, we were not "together" any more.

URBANA (AUGUST 1981–JUNE 1985)

A week later, we moved into a two-bedroom apartment in Green Acres, the university student family housing in Urbana. It was surrounded by green lawns, crabapple trees, cornfields from horizon to horizon, and one artificial hill for skiing in the wintertime. Around us we could hear any language in the world, and we could see children of all races playing together outside.

"I loved the place."

We all fell in love with the place and with the university. You made good friends with children from many different ethnic backgrounds. In fact, more than anyone that I've ever known, you became "color-blind" with regard to people.

I believe that this exposure, at such a young age, prompted your development of the acute sensitivity that you showed for any form of discrimination against people. For example, you were extremely bothered by teachers' stereotyping girls as weaker in comparison to boys. You saw it as an expression of discrimination.

"It was sexism!"

I agree. Years later you called yourself a feminist.

One early experience of living in a multicultural and multilingual neighborhood is forever engraved in my memory. We had been in Green Acres only a week. From our kitchen window, I watched you playing with our Korean neighbors' 3-year-old boy. It appeared as though the two of you were having a very lively conversation. I saw you using your hands a lot and heard him speaking Korean. He raised his voice as if he was trying to make you understand what he was telling you. I could hear you telling him, in fluent baby Hebrew, that your name was Gili and what your brother's name was. There was not a silent moment between the two of you. When the little boy's mother called him home, you came rushing in. Breathless from excitement, you told me of your admiration for your new friend, "Ima, hayeled haze medaber Anglit kol kach tov!" (This boy speaks English so well!) I wondered what that child told his mother about your "English," Gili.

On August 25, 1981, your third birthday, you started your first American school, the Unicorn Day-Care.

"There I met Meera."

Yes, your lifelong Israeli friend. You made other friends too, but Meera helped you adjust to school. Until you learned to speak English, she used to translate for your teachers and for you. This happened within 3 weeks! We found out that you spoke English when your father and I came to pick you up from school one day. You were sitting on the floor with your back to us, and you couldn't see us. We heard a teacher calling you—"Gili!"—and you responding, "What?" Then I called you—"Gili!"—and you responded to my voice. Without turning around to look at me, you said in Hebrew, "Ma?" Evidently, you had learned to distinguish between the "hard L" that is used in pronouncing Gili in English and the "soft L" used in Hebrew.

"Parents are not supposed to speak English, only Hebrew," you insisted back then.

"It confuses the child," you told us with some resentment. "Only teachers are supposed to speak English."

You are laughing now, but then you were very serious. You sounded as if you were stating a universal wish on behalf of all bilingual children.

"We used to laugh whenever you told that story."

When you were 5 years old, your father and I thought it would be a good idea to teach you how to read and write in English. I have a recording of you reading your first words in English. You could hardly stop hollering for sheer joy. You giggled in total elation and happiness.

Only two months later, on January 28, 1984, you read an entire story in English and explained it to us in Hebrew. For the rest of your life you were a reader. You loved books and you showed a real talent for learning new languages. Painting, drawing, and sculpting were some other of your pronounced talents. I was very proud of your artistic talents. Guy, your grandfathers, your father and I have all painted at different times in our life. Seeing your blossoming talent made me explode with pride and love.

"You hung my pictures everywhere."

Yes, and you loved it. Our apartment was decorated with Guy's drawings, too. There was not a day that you did not create art. We have had a constant exhibition of your artwork in every available corner of the house until this day, and I will for the rest of my life.

You shared a room with Guy. You liked that arrangement, but he didn't. He was already 12 years old, and he wanted more privacy. Do you remember what his common complaints were?

"Yes, that I am looking at him, or that I am breathing on him. He was right, Mommy. I did that sometimes, because I wanted to get back at him. But at other times, I did it because I just wanted to be close to my big brother."

You always admired him.

"That's easy, he is so smart! Ima, do you remember, how my brother, the chess champion, tried to teach me chess?"

Yes, I remember that. At one point you got tired of his telling you what to do and how to play, so you told him that "enough is enough."

"I told him that from now on we are going to play by my rules, not his."

I remember; Guy looked puzzled but amused. "Chess rules are universal," he said. "I didn't make them up. Therefore, you cannot play by your rules."

You were not convinced. You shook your head in disagreement and said, "Uh-uh, I can make up my own rules, and now we will play chess by my rules."

"What are these rules?" he asked skeptically.

You answered with authority: "They are changeable rules. I change them whenever I want to."

And Guy played by your "changeable" rules. You are smiling but I am crying. If we could have stayed in those moments forever, maybe the horror would not have happened.

"Mommy, please don't cry. Tell me more."

I'll try, Booba sheli. Another thing you did with Guy, whenever he allowed you, was to help him to deliver newspapers in Green Acres. You were eager to help him. On that job, he was "the boss"; you followed his rules.

You behaved the same way at school and on the playground—always ready to help without being asked. There were times when I was afraid that you would be taken advantage of, but you were not concerned at all.

"Mommy, I loved to help, and I did what I liked to do. You should have not been worried about me."

I worried about everything when it came to you and Guy, but particularly you.

We celebrated your third birthday in the Unicorn Day-Care. It was a happy day—you started to express yourself in English, and you felt increasingly better in your new surroundings. The teachers loved you, and you bonded with them. The beginning of your acquisition of English signaled the end of

Gili at age six, helping her brother in delivering newspapers

your Hebrew. From then on, you would talk at home in a blended language of Hebrew–English that gradually became English–Hebrew. We wanted you to retain Hebrew; therefore, we insisted on using mainly Hebrew when talking to you and when teaching you to read and write in Hebrew.

"I enjoyed being able to speak in more than one language."

Later, in school, you added French, German, and Spanish. You intended to learn these languages more thoroughly as you grew up. A typical example of the way you spoke in this new blended language was, "Ani lo scared of the water; ani rotza shehu yistakel at me" (I am not scared of the water; I want him to look at me). This you said once, referring to your swimming instructor, who did not pay special attention to you while instructing a whole group of children.

"I loved swimming, too."

Yes, swimming was another of the skills that you learned a few years later.

"But this time, Guy was my instructor."

He was an excellent teacher to an excellent student. He really helped you to discover the joy of swimming well. Another source of delight for you was the snow. You had never seen snow before we moved to Illinois. For the rest of your life, you loved playing in the snow.

"I loved to taste it."

And you loved to roll in it. And even after your skin had turned blue and purple, you wouldn't stop playing.

With an angelic smile you would say to me, "Ima, this white blanket makes me feel so peaceful." And as though God had listened to your heart, He covered Houston with a "white blanket" just a few days before the accident. The last pictures we took were of you playing in the snow early in the morning. You wore a red coat over your nightgown. You were elated then. Your giggles still echo in my ears. It reminded me of other cries of joy in other snows way back in Green Acres. I can almost hear your laughter coming over the snow-covered hill.

You took great joy in any playful movement, in dancing or in running.

"I loved to play and to dress up in disguises that I had made."

As shy as you were, you enjoyed performing, especially if I was your audience. Later in your life, you used to alter your room or parts of our home and enact whole scenes, as if you were performing on a stage.

When you started kindergarten and first grade at Luther Elementary School in Urbana, you had a rare opportunity to study in a school where the students were from every nation in the world. The teachers were open and receptive to cultural differences. You blossomed in that environment.

Your teachers became role models for tolerance of others and a lack of prejudice. You yourself became a model student and a role model for others.

"I wrote my first letter to you, Ima."

You wrote:

Dear Mom
    I like when I am sick and you take
    care of me.
        Love   Gili

"It sounds pitiful. I must have felt really sorry for myself that day."

It was the first of many more letters and love notes you would write in the years to come.

"Sometimes I hid them under your blanket, on your pillow, among the leaves of a hanging plant, or across your bedroom door, so that my love note would be the first thing you saw in the morning and the last thing you saw at night."

How much I miss those love notes—and those sweet hands that wrote them and put them out for me to find. I'm choking. It's hard to catch my breath now, as I look at them. Here is one that you wrote when I was sick.

"There are so many pictures from our visit to Israel. I wish we could show them all. I would visit Israel one more time, two years later, no?"

Yes, Googi, and that would be your last visit, my child. Nobody in our family, except my sister, saw you older than at age 7. How sad that they never came to visit us here. In the summer of 1983, when you were 5 years old, we went to visit our family in Israel.

"I had sweet and sad memories from that visit. I had a feeling that it would take a very long time until I saw them again."

And you were right, my love.

A love note from Gili, left at night on my pillow:
Sweet dreams

Another love note and a humorous
drawing from Gili: Feel better!

At the time of our visit, our small family was still intact, although the
drifting apart of your father, myself, and Guy had already started. I felt
the signs, but I was too scared to admit them. This admission came a few
years later. Maybe you felt the signs, too, and that is why you and I clung
so to each other—as if to strengthen each other against the impending
breakup of our family.

Two years after the visit to Israel, in the summer of 1985, I had completed my doctorate at the University of Illinois and was about to start my
internship at Southern Illinois University at Carbondale. Your father had
completed his doctorate and was looking for a job in Israel. Although Guy
and you both loved your schools and did very well there, you had no choice
but to follow me to Carbondale. Your father said that he could not take
care of both of you, and I felt that I could not live without my children. So,
your father stayed in Urbana to work until he found a job in Israel, and the
three of us moved to Carbondale for one year. We were sad about the separation but also relieved and excited about the change.

"Before we moved, I remember that I lost my first tooth."

Aha. And you smiled proudly. Incidentally, the first tooth you lost was
also your first baby tooth.

"I felt so grown up in my first school year—I was ready to start second grade."

CARBONDALE (JUNE 1985–JULY 1986)

In June of 1985 we drove down from Urbana to Carbondale—only four hours of driving, but a world of difference. June in Urbana was the beginning of spring. In Carbondale it felt like the middle of summer.

"We loved the lakes and the forest that surrounded us."

But we did not like the cultural isolation. Guy felt like an outsider at school. He was allowed to skip a grade and graduate at age 16, after only 3 years of high school. It seemed to me that this would give him some satisfaction, so I made a special effort to convince the school authorities that he was capable of this accelerated schedule. Guy did not disappoint them in that respect, although they were disappointed that he preferred chess to football. Actually, both of you handled the cultural "shock" with humor and courage that was inspiring to me.

When you were in second grade at Blue Lake, I remember your coming home from school one day and, with a puzzled expression, asking me why we did not believe in Jesus since he was "Jewish and was such a good person." You then added that you were upset because some kids at school had accused *you* of killing Jesus. Almost in tears you asked me, "Mommy, did we do it?"

It did not take much to explain to you our beliefs and to convince you that we did not kill Jesus or anybody else. You smiled at me in relief.

"Uh-uh, I didn't want to get involved in conflicts. I preferred peace. I was proud to be Jewish and an Israeli. I respected their beliefs and I expected them to respect mine. I just wanted to make sure that we don't go around killing people."

*   *   *

Our adjustment was not easy. I had to work long hours on my internship in a nonsupportive environment. At least in the beginning, we felt isolated and lonely. Although we found an Israeli couple who later became our friends, we still felt isolated from former friends and we were lonely for your father. For the first few months, your father used to come to visit us once a week, but then he got a job in Israel and left us for more than a year. In retrospect, I think that on some unconscious level your father and I must have known that our marriage was doomed.

More than once you came running home upset, hurting and crying because some children doubted that you had a father at all. They said that you were lying, that you had made it up. For your friends to accuse you of lying was extremely painful, because you prided yourself on trying to be truthful all the time.

"I remember, I used to ask you in tears: Mommy, how do I know that I have a daddy? I hear only a voice on the telephone; maybe it's somebody else?"

I hurt with you. Our partial solution was to take your father for a long walk in the neighborhood whenever he came to visit, so all the children could see you together. You and I used to take walks to the lake near our house or to the woods.

"I will never forget one of those walks in the woods. It was a sunny Saturday morning. We were walking hand in hand, chatting and picking some wildflowers, when from the corner of my eye I noticed it: a snake!"

Yes, a snake. I was terrified. You know how scared I am of snakes.

"But, Mommy, it was a baby snake."

That's exactly what you said then when I urged you to run—I was ready to fly!

"I didn't want to run. I wanted to follow it. Does it have a Mommy and Daddy, I asked you, and where does it live? You, Mommy, said that you hoped it was an orphan! And you pulled me away from the woods. I thought that it was fun, but you didn't."

*   *   *

On September 3, 1985, when you were 6 years old and in second grade in Blue Lake Elementary School, you started writing a diary. There are several references to your father's visits in it. In carefully drawn letters and with cute spelling mistakes, you wrote:

September 19, 1985
    Today my momy is coming to the open house and I am glad. and I love you momy.

September 20, 1985
    My dad is coming today to my house and he is leving Wenday. I know my spelling wards.

September 23, 1985
    Yesterday I got a hair cut. My dad is going to pick me up at the bus.

I apologize for reading your diary. Please forgive me—I have always respected your privacy.

"Ima, I understand why you did it, and it's OK."

Your diary reflects your character and your inner growth so well. From the very first page, you come across as a child who took school assignments seriously. The teacher asked you to write a diary, so you did—every day. My joy was in seeing how much you enjoyed writing the diary.

"I felt that writing a diary was like being a grown-up. Since then I always liked diaries. And when I was 10, and read the diary of Anne Frank, she became one of my heroines."

Over time, your writing style, the content, and your handwriting changed. From a little 6-year-old who reported every activity you did or planned to do, you matured into a 7-year-old who was capable of expressing her feelings. I am grateful for all that you wrote because, in spite of my pain, you remind me how well you adjusted to it all—how capable you were of finding happiness in the midst of misery. This is another important lesson you taught me, my love.

While reading your diary, page after page, I came across a reference to Erica, who was your best friend in Carbondale. One of my fondest memories of that time is related to a baby born in Erica's family. Do you remember? I asked you: "Is the baby a boy or a girl?" And you answered patiently:

"We don't know yet. It's not a boy or a girl. It's only a baby."

It still makes me laugh (and cry).

*   *   *

You liked to illustrate your writings, and you became a gifted cartoonist.

"I loved to imitate animals' expressions."

Yes, every animal "talked" to you, and you expressed it all in your stories, paintings, cartoons, and sculptures. Here is one typical drawing that you made much later, when you were about 10 years old and I was already married to Norm. You can see, in this funny drawing of our family, that we are all aliens, hugging each other. The two Kagans are Norm and myself, and the one Klein between us is you. What was Shelly, your dog, with her amused expression, gigantic ears, and wiggling tail?

"Oh, she was a Klein curious [a little curious], of course."

"I especially liked to draw Shelly doing her routine things: scratching, 'manicuring' her claws, begging for food—"

So, here is the one and only Shelly.

You earned excellent grades in everything that you studied. To Guy's delight (he is the real mathematician in our family), you discovered your love for math.

"Uh-huh, some of my best times were spent with my brother teaching me tricks and shortcuts in math. Although he used to protest that arithmetic is not real math, it was enough for me."

Do you remember what else you studied in Carbondale?

The Kagan family and one Klein as aliens

Gili's impressions of Shelly, her pet

"Ballet!"

For a while you and I went together to a ballet school run by a friend. We didn't last too long there. We both felt frustrated trying to please our teacher. We suspected that she felt we danced with enthusiasm but with limited talent.

"Aha. But Mommy, we were not so pathetic a year later in Athens. I really enjoyed dancing then."

Me, too.

CHAPTER 3

New Adjustments: Athens, Georgia (July 1986–August 1988)

When you, Guy, and I left Carbondale and headed southeast to Athens, Georgia (your brother was our driver), we did not know that we were going to experience the agonizing and bitter breakup of our family there.

Our move did not start too smoothly—for 2 weeks we were without furniture, your father was in Israel, and my job as professor at the university was demanding. But, at least in the beginning, Athens for me was the South that I had read about in books—spread out lazily on wooded hills, covered with magnificent magnolia trees, and oozing nostalgia of better days (pre–Civil War, of course)—provincial and conservative for sure, but charming. Only later did it become stifling. Once again we all experienced a cultural shock. The first question that I was asked regarding my foreign accent was: "Are you a Yankee?" ("Yes," I responded, "a Mediterranean Yankee.") You, my love, had a similar experience to mine, remember?

"Yes, Mommy. If in Carbondale I was accused of killing Jesus, in Georgia, during my first week at school, some children came over to me and stated with much authority that I was a Yankee (I came to Georgia from Illinois—Yankee land—and besides, anybody who spoke with a different accent from the local one was considered a Yankee) and therefore had killed Southerners! As soon as they found out that I was Jewish and an Israeli, I was accused, once again, of killing not only Jesus but also Ayrabs (they meant Arabs). After my initial shock, I thought it was funny. These children must have been quite scared of me, with all these killings in my backpack! My protests and explanations didn't help to change their minds, so I shrugged and laughed."

I remember that, Mommile. I also remember that one day you came home from school crying not only because some kids were continuing to give you a hard time about these "killings" but also because you were having difficulty understanding your teacher's accent.

"I felt hurt and confused, because my teacher kept correcting my 'Yankee accent' all the time."

Those first days in Athens were tough. But I knew that your adjustment crisis was over when one day you left home to play with a friend (as usual, you made friends very quickly) and, while waving goodbye to me, said in a giggle, "Baah, Momma!" You said it in a perfect "Georgian" accent. We cracked up laughing. From then on, whenever you were in an especially affectionate mood you would speak or write me love notes in "Southern." I loved it—my Israeli Yankee converted to a Southerner.

Three months after the three of us settled down (you in third grade at Gables school, your brother as a freshman in math at the University of Georgia, and I as a University professor), your father joined us. It seemed that the three of us had already overcome our adjustment crisis; however, your father had not. He arrived from Israel with new ideas (new to me) and wishes to live an alternative lifestyle, with less commitment and less emotional involvement, as he told me. I was devastated. I did not expect that. After more than a year of living (and drifting) apart, I had hoped that we would be more emotionally involved with each other, not less involved, and more committed to our life together. My fantasy was to patch up the cracks and tears in our lives and to have a renewed beginning. I soon realized that he and I had drifted apart too much. We struggled to stay together for another year, but by the summer it was clear that we would divorce. Your father responded by contesting custody. We all endured tremendous suffering, but especially you.

I worked hard not to let any of these new developments harm you and your brother, but of course you were hurt. You started complaining about stomachaches. You looked tired, your hair lost its shine, and you lost your appetite. Every time I looked at you, my heart cried. I felt so helpless and overwhelmed. There were moments that I was angry at you. I resented the pain I saw in your eyes—a constant reminder of the pain I felt I was causing you.

"I told Aba [daddy] that I would run away if he forced me to live with him."

I know that, my love, and my heart was bleeding when I heard you saying that. I knew how painful it was for you to say those words to your father—you loved him very much—and how painful it was for him to hear them. I also wanted to run away to the end of the world, away from this unbearable pain. At times I wished I could close my eyes and disappear or never wake up. I could not do it then; I cannot do it now. The pain, the shame, the guilt are my constant companions.

To our shock (including your father's), the judge awarded your father custody; apparently, a mother with a career cannot be a good mother—but a father can. This was the first time that I felt as though the world had collapsed on me. I felt that I'd die if you were taken away from me. The three of us cried—you and I clinging to each other in despair, Guy keeping some distance. To my surprise, he decided to support us, and the three of us agreed to confront your father that same afternoon. After long hours of screaming, crying, begging, and reasoning, your father agreed that we would go back to the judge the next day and ask him to reverse his order—that you would live with me and he would have visitation rights, but it would be called "joint custody." The judge changed the order the following day and, looking into my eyes, said, "I wish you well." Since then, I have sometimes wondered if this judge ever understood the full meaning of his decisions—the first one and the second one. Didn't he know that he was opening another channel for continuing legal battles? The judge knew that your father was going back to Israel, and he must have known that there was no reciprocity between Israeli and American courts. So how were we supposed to interpret what "joint custody" meant under these circumstances?

I would have given my life to have you with me, legal battles or no legal battles.

All of that concentrated suffering took place toward our second year in Athens. Looking back, I know now that it was an introduction to what was awaiting us only a year and a half later. It was only a preparation for your ultimate separation from us, from me. But then, I still had you to comfort me, and you had me to comfort you. Nobody will ever be able to comfort me any more. Who, my love, is comforting you now?

*   *   *

I said earlier that during these 2 years in Athens you taught me one of the most important lessons of my life. You taught me that the search for meaning can be done in joy. You tried to show me that it was possible to find joy and even happiness in the midst of sorrow and disaster.

You told me time and again whenever I became disenchanted with life: "Ima, nothing is only bad. If you only look closer you'll see that every 'bad' has also something 'good.'" I saw you living up to your premise. I don't know how. I am still learning to find and to feel joy or happiness. I am afraid that I may fail this lesson.

Engraved on my mind are your laughter, your little dances of happiness, your love letters, your artwork glowing in vibrant colors, your jokes. Remember the time you painted colorful faces on all the eggs in the refrigerator? They looked like a row of lunatic clowns staring me right in the eye.

"Yes, and you didn't want to use those eggs."

How could I? They were a work of art. Could I eat art?

I remember the heart-to-heart conversations we used to have about anything in the world—religion, femininity. You started developing a strong sense of identity, partially through identifying with me, and pride in who you were.

When having to write a sentence using the word *abhor*, you wrote the following, which expressed your (and my) strong feminist identity:

> "My feelings are *abhor* when it comes to racial [you meant "racism"] and treating women differently than men."

You tended to use your homework assignments as an outlet to express your views on different issues—racism, human rights, and so on.

We talked about abused and neglected children. Your heart went out to the helpless and disadvantaged, especially children. Remember Barbara, your classmate? You brought her home so we could feed her and dress her up.

"Well, I could tell that she was very poor."

You expressed your worries, anxieties, fears, humor, and love for all of us and for others, not only in our conversations but also in your artwork.

"I wrote stories and illustrated them."

You also wrote silly poems with rhymes. Here is an example:

I've got a shrew
with a flue
on my blue shoe
with a screw
with some glue
but it can't stop it
because I am about to drop it
on my blue ue ue
S h o o o e !
By: Gili Klein

"Yes, but I was not really proud of them. I was just playing with words."

I know—so what? Your poems became better in time. What was important was that you were not afraid to express yourself, and this was how you developed your creativity. You also wrote short stories, illustrated them, and put them together into booklets.

"And I wrote plays. Remember *The Sleeping Beauty*?"

I remember, and I have them all. Did I ever tell you that I used to do the same things when I was your age? I liked to write plays, and I enjoyed putting them on stage with the neighborhood kids.

"No, Ima, I don't remember you telling me that. It's funny to imagine you as a little girl my age."

There are so many things that I never took the opportunity to tell you, my child. When I thought that you and I still had a lifetime ahead of us, when I thought that we still had a tomorrow, I used to put off telling you until I would have time. Now, my love, I finally have time, but where are you?

"But I hear you, Mommy. My heart listens to yours, and I don't need ears or a physical heart to feel you."

How much I wish with all my heart that this is true.

*   *   *

The first year in Athens was bittersweet. I told you some of the "bitter"; now let me recall the "sweet." As I look at your pictures in the album, I see you holding Shelly, your puppy, in your arms. It was my idea to get you a pet, to help you in your adjustment to our new home. You and I thought that we preferred a pet that nobody else wanted.

"I fell in love with Shelly from first sight. From the moment we locked eyes at the kennel of the Humane Society, I knew that we were meant for each other. You would call it 'fate,' Ima. She was so tiny and funny with her black patches around her smart-looking eyes, her tiny little ears folded downward, and her wiggling fuzzy tail. I asked you, Mommy, what kind of breed she was. Remember what you answered?"

I said, "all kinds."

"And I laughed, because she really looked like a mix of every breed in the world."

We decided to name her Shelly. It means "mine" in Hebrew, but it also sounds like a girl's name in English.

"Shelly and I became inseparable."

She mourned for you, Gili, for a long time.

"I know, Mommy, that you believe that Shelly grieves for me. You may want to write a children's book about mourning and use your observations of Shelly's mourning. You know what Norm would have said to you: 'Be productive!'"

What choice do I have when you start quoting Norm?

You took your responsibility for your dog very seriously, as you took any other responsibility in your life. You checked out books about dogs from the library. You educated yourself and us about how to raise a dog, and you were very devoted to her until your last day.

"But after a while, I couldn't take care of both Shelly and my mice, Avram and Vice. I had too much homework to do. So I had to let them go."

And you shed many tears when you and Norm walked to the field across the street and let the "couple" go. There wasn't a day that you didn't ask in a trembling voice whether they were still alive or not. You regretted it many times. You were a "softy" when it came to what you identified as "helplessness" in animals, young children, or old people. You especially loved "babies" of all kinds—human or animal.

*   *   *

When we were still with your father and your brother, we took several trips; one of them was to Key West, Florida. Do you remember what was special about that trip, Gili?

"Uh-huh, I remember that trip very well. I borrowed several books from the library—grown-up books about the beaches of Florida, the shells, fish, flowers, and trees. And during the whole trip I was busy reading and telling you what I read."

When we arrived, we were tickled by your seriousness and by how well informed you actually were. You were in third grade then. How amusing it was listening to your "mini-lectures." I was so proud of you, I could hardly contain myself. We could see that you were a serious student and a scientist at heart. What a combination of talents and character—it hurts so badly thinking of the magnitude of your death.

One day you came home from school—you were a fourth-grader. You could hardly contain yourself. You hopped from foot to foot in excitement. All giggles, you told us that you "went to visit today the grandma that was chosen for me in the nursing home."

"I liked that grandma, but she kept forgetting my name. I told her a story; who I was, what I was doing in school, and things like that. And she nodded her head and smiled to me. She was really sweet. But by the time I was through telling her my story, she had already forgotten my name."

We all laughed when you so vividly mimicked the old grandma asking you over and over, "what's your name, you sweet little thing?"

"I wished that my teacher would have selected a grandma with a better memory for me, but I like that grandma anyway."

In Athens, as in the other places that we lived in, you loved school, you loved your teachers—especially those of your third and fourth grades. Remember the giraffe you made for one of your teachers because you knew that she collected giraffes? You also used to decorate the margins of your notebooks with miniature illustrations, just to make your teacher smile.

Your teachers rewarded your efforts.

There wasn't a day that you didn't come home with one "medal" or another. Both teachers and children loved you. You attended a special program for gifted children (the first of others to come), and you enjoyed the challenge.

Your report cards continued to be excellent in spite of your anxieties and the uncertainties in your life then.

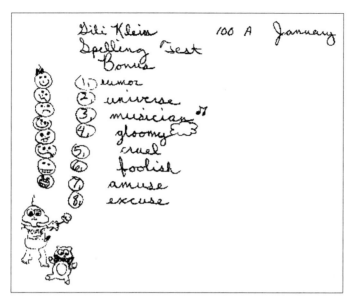

An illustrated spelling test in third grade

I could not figure out where you got that positive energy from. What kept you so optimistic that "everything will be fine," as you often used to say to me?

"But, Ima, I felt loved by all of you. And I loved you all. I knew deep in my heart that all of you would protect me. And as long as there was more love between us than hate, I knew that everything would work out for the best. I believed in what I used to tell you, Mommy—it's more important to be happy than to hold on to what does not make you happy anymore."

How did you become so mature and wise, I used to wonder. I had to remind myself that this mature person was only 9 years old! And like any other 9-year-old, you were playful and funny.

"Ima, do you remember how I used to surprise you with indoor picnics on our verandah?"

How can I forget that? You know, since your death my memory has changed drastically. From having an excellent memory I've gone to possessing (or does it possess me) a sieve-like memory—I remember with acute clarity everything about you—what you sounded like and looked like and felt and did. These memories are important to me. The rest are like islands that I bump into occasionally, floating in an ocean of forgetfulness.

"Don't be sad, Mommy. This may change, too. You took on the job of 'the one who records and remembers' in order to be a constant reminder of me."

Yes. I felt that those who knew you, at least some of them, were making active efforts not to include you in their lives any more.

"So you had to become the reminder that I lived and that my life was meaningful."

True.

"Well, one day you may realize that you achieved your goal of keeping my memory alive, and then you may let other memories be retained in your 'sieve.' I don't think that your memory is so bad. I think that you remember better what you think is relevant or important to your life."

Yes, and they are different things than were important to me in the past.

Sometimes, I would knock on your door and you would answer in a deep voice, "Come in." You would sit on the floor, dressed up as a fortune-teller, and tell me my future. How come we couldn't foresee your future, my child?

When the magnolia trees where in bloom, you loved to surprise me with a specially selected flower that you put in a vase. You knew that the picking of magnolia flowers was not allowed in our neighborhood. When I reminded you of that, you smiled in mischief and said in a Georgian accent, "Ah do only what's goood fo ma Momma."

Gili at almost age ten, with a magnolia flower

"Mommy, Mommy, do you remember the Oofoogee Village?"

Of course I remember. One afternoon I woke up from a short nap to find the whole apartment transformed into "an African village." I hardly recognized you either. You were painted all over your face and body; even your glasses had some interesting figures painted on them (who ever saw a nearsighted cannibal?). You were naked from your waist up, and you lifted your hair up. You tied it up with a bone-like object. You looked like one happy cannibal. For a whole week we talked the Oofoogee language; you kept making up new words in the middle of our conversations. We ate Oofoogee food and we even dreamt Oofoogee.

One day you surprised me when you asked me to hurry up and take a picture of you. That was unusual. I knew that you were "cooking up" something. And indeed, I almost fainted when I saw you—actually, I first noticed a huge chest, then big blue eyes winking at me, then I saw the biggest smile in the world. I couldn't miss it—your lips had the brightest lipstick that I had ever seen (where did you get it?). "I'm Dolly Parton," you said, "do you like it?" We both started laughing so hard that the camera fell out of my hands. We collapsed laughing in each other's arms, but nevertheless, I managed to take a picture of you posing as "sweet Dolly Parton," as you called her.

Your ninth birthday was not very happy. Your father and I lived apart, but on that day we all made a special effort to overcome our animosity and

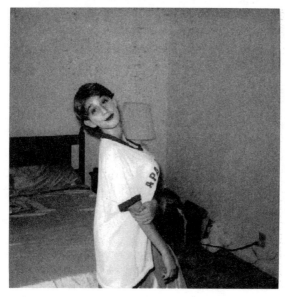

Gili as "sweet Dolly Parton"

celebrate your life. You received many gifts from all of us and from Norm. Your brother gave you a special birthday card that you cherished, as you did anything that he gave you.

Had we known then that you would have only two more birthdays to celebrate, would we have changed anything?

"I was sort of happy then. It was kind of happy and kind of sad, but on my tenth birthday, I was happier. Although I missed Daddy a little bit."

A year later, on August 25, 1988, we celebrated your tenth birthday in Savannah, Georgia, just a day before Norm and I got married.

But before the custody battle ended "happily," you and I went to Houston, for a visit and a job interview. We had a joyous time visiting. It was such a relief after the intense pain we had suffered in Athens. We were both hungry for kindness and compassion. Norm gave us more than that—he loved us. One of the places we visited on our trip to Houston was heaven on earth: a store of stuffed animals! Norm knew how much you loved stuffed animals, especially "mommies and babies," so he took us there to indulge ourselves, but also to shop. We later surprised you with a giant panda bear who could be unzipped to store things inside its belly. You loved to carry it with you for sleepover. You found another surprise—a baby panda who rested inside the bear's zipped-up belly. So here we are, embracing in total happiness, on "heaven's" floor.

"Don't forget Mommy, the beautiful flowers that Norm used to send us every week for a whole year, in Athens. One bouquet was for you and one was for me. We felt like two elegant ladies from some novel. We loved the colorful flower arrangements, the surprise; and it made us feel so special."

Do you remember this badge?:

American Psychological Association
Gili Klein, Houston, TX
    96th Annual Meeting, Atlanta, GA.

"Yes. I came with you to Atlanta for a conference, and Norm got me that badge. It made me feel like a real 'professional.' I couldn't wait to become a psychologist myself. Meanwhile, I enjoyed the attention. But I also loved staying in the hotel with you."

Me, too, my love. I would give my life to go back to that moment when I could still feel your kiss.

A few weeks after the custody arrangements and the divorce were final, Norm arrived in Athens and helped us move to Houston. Guy and his girlfriend at the time, as well as my sister (who had flown in from Israel for my wedding), helped us pack. On August 20, at 8:00 in the morning, we

Gili and I embracing in "stuffed animals heaven"

The kiss

were all packed in my car. Norm; my sister; you, "armed" with books and crayons and paper; Shelly, your doggy; Avram and Vice, your mice—we all started our journey to our new home. It took us two days to get to Houston. Two days later we were on our way back to Georgia, for the wedding. This time we took a plane, to romantic Savannah. The wedding seemed like a happy ending to a nightmare.

When I look at one particular wedding picture, the one where I am standing between Norm and you, all of us smiling, you in your beautiful white dress, I choke: I am surrounded by ghosts.

"Don't cry, Mommy sheli. We are friendly ghosts, who like to make house calls."

Oh, I love you so much. You got plenty of attention and gifts, but of course I knew that you felt some sadness, too. You looked so radiant and beautiful. My heart skipped a beat every time I looked at you. You handled yourself with so much grace, and at the same time, you were still my little baby, just a kid.

Gili, on our wedding day in Savannah, Georgia

You whispered to me, "I loved the wedding. Everything was so beautiful and romantic. I wish my wedding would be like that."

I wish that, too, my love, but it wasn't meant to be I guess. On your tenth birthday, just a day before the wedding, you looked like a beautiful butterfly, glowing in yellows and pastels, and so fragile. Whenever I think of summer, hopes and fragile happiness, I see you as you were on that day, etched in my mind.

CHAPTER 4

A Promising New Life: Houston, Texas (August 1988–January 3, 1990)

After the wedding we settled down into a routine of school and work. You were a fifth-grader now at Rainbow Elementary.

During the first 6 months after we moved to Houston, I stayed at home. I wanted to be with you as much as possible, and I also needed time to heal from the bitter custody battle. Nothing was over yet. We were still entangled with lawyers. I was ill. Norm and I anticipated that you would be in crisis, too, from the many changes that you had experienced that last year: a messy divorce and custody feud, my remarriage, moving to a new place, your father's departure to Israel, and Guy's detachment from all of us. But the crisis never happened. On the contrary, you thrived and blossomed.

"But, Mommy, why a crisis? I loved it here: the new home, Norm, the new people I met. Everybody was kind and nice to me. I felt such a relief. No knots in my stomach anymore. No rashes on my skin. No waking up in the morning and not being sure where I am—At Daddy's? At your house? I felt secure and loved. I could put Athens and all last year behind me. Sure, I missed Daddy and my brother, but I knew that I'd see them again. And I had you! And I had Norm—and a whole new life ahead of me. I was excited more than anxious. I couldn't wait to start school and make new friends."

Yes, that was your attitude—look at the bright side, don't dwell on the past, focus on what you have and are blessed with. And you made new friends. Within a week, we had girls over to our house and we started driving you around town to visit your new friends. This was how I got to know Houston. You did very well in school, too. Here, too, you were in the gifted program, and you truly loved the challenge. It felt as though you smiled at Life and Life smiled back at you.

An incident comes to my mind while looking at the album pictures. I recall that one day you told me about your math teacher in fifth grade, Dr. Hunter, and how much the other children were scared of him and thought that he was mean. I asked you if you were scared of him, too, and what you thought of him. Remember what you said?

"I said that I was not scared of him. I respected him. I think that he was the best teacher that I ever had. I also didn't think that he was mean. I thought that he was a puppy. I saw him with his baby girl, and he was the softest Daddy that you could imagine. I didn't believe that a person who was so sweet to his child could be mean to other children."

That was you, Gili. Always trusting the good nature of people. Always seeing beyond the surface. And always optimistic.

One of the main events in school was the track racing. You were one of the better runners. You discovered a new talent. It amused me how much we were alike. I was also a good runner at your age. On one rainy and steamy day, Norm and I went to watch you running.

"Yes, and I was miserable. I couldn't finish the race. I was out of breath before the finish line. It had never happened to me before, and when I caught my breath, I asked you, Ima, if this was how it was going to be from now on, because I was becoming a teenager."

No, I reassured you. You were just tired. You would still be able to run as a teenager or as a woman. You, my little athlete, remembered only the defeat; but I remember your joy in running side by side with your class-mates when it was their turn to run, encouraging those who were falling behind. I saw you laughing and joking as you tried to instill confidence in them. And when it was your turn to run, you ran like a gazelle, touching–not touching the ground. The audience applauded and your friends hollered; they surrounded you and encouraged you when they saw you were starting to fall behind. I was hurting with you when you didn't make it to the finish line. Your run was a short one, Yalda sheli, but what a mag-nificent run it was!

You bonded with your new friends. I especially remember the inten-sity of your caring about your friends—old and new. You very often asked me questions about issues that troubled them—issues such as relationships with parents and parents' reactions to bad grades.

"I was so lucky that you never punished me for getting a bad grade. You always said that the most important thing was to truly do the best I could and that was good enough."

Yes, but you also never had bad grades, so who knows. One of your dilemmas was whether you should offer to help a girl whom you thought needed help but who didn't think so herself. You concluded that she could not be helped as long as she didn't acknowledge that she needed help. Re-member the conversation about an older girlfriend who had a stepfather like you did? You told me that you asked her how she was doing with her stepfather. Not because you were nosy but because, "I wanted to learn from her experience how to deal with a stepfather," you said. You were disap-pointed when that girl refused to talk about her relationship with him.

"I felt so sorry for her. I thought that she didn't have a good relationship with her stepfather. I'd try to do better with mine."

And you did.

When discussing your friends' problems with me, you never mentioned their names.

"It was because I didn't want to betray their trust."

Gili, you would have made an excellent therapist; not only because of your sensitivity, caring, and compassion for people, but also because of your high morals and ethics.

You were especially involved with Lili, Doris, Anna, Delila, Danielle, and Rikki. There were long phone calls every day. Norm was concerned that we might need to get you a separate line, and meanwhile he started monitoring the length of time you spent on the phone. I was more amused than annoyed—my baby was becoming a teenager.

You loved funny hats. This one was your special attire to pick up our mail from the mailbox.

You made jewelry from clay with Rikki: earrings, bracelets, pins for me, and a tie holder for Norm. I see jewelry like that sold in stores. You made miniature sculptures from clay or paper; I could hear you tip-toeing on your way to the kitchen at 6:00 in the morning, so as not to wake us

Gili, wearing her favorite funny hat, and Shelly

up, to bake in the oven the latest clay sculpture you had made the night before for us, for me, or for your friends. You never forgot to add a loving note with your gift. I noticed the intensity of your artwork especially during what ended up being the last 4 months of your life: It seemed as though you created something new every day! Almost every morning there was a drawing, a sculpture, or at least a love note from you. I often wonder: Why?

Remember the miniature red sports car that you made and gave me for my birthday? And being considerate of Norm's feelings, you sculpted an accurate replica of his favorite antique car. You even painted the wrapping paper in bright rainbow colors.

Children as well as other parents became attached to you. Parents used to call me up and ask if I could send you over because "Gili has such a good influence on our children" or because "when Gili comes into our house, she brings in light." It warmed my heart to hear that, and I was so proud to be your mother. After you died, Lili published a poem about you in her Sunday School magazine, written in Hebrew. The poem is called "The Worst Day of My Life." That was the day that you, my love, died. Three years later, Lili published an article about you in her high school newspaper. She titled the article "Her Body Is Gone, but Her Heart and Soul Live On." I was very touched by Lili's writings.

Gili's gift to us—two miniature sport cars made of clay

I look at the pictures taken on your graduation from fifth grade at Rainbow Elementary School. You looked sad even when you were smiling with Doris; it was painful to say goodbye to friends and beloved teachers.

"It was hard to become a grown-up. I didn't want to grow up."

When I think of your graduation from fifth grade, your 4 months in sixth grade come to mind, as vivid as if it was just earlier today; every time I looked out the window, I could still see you in my mind, standing at the curve under the oak tree, early in the morning, with your heavy backpack bending your whole body forward, waiting for the schoolbus to arrive. You were so anxious to get to school—sixth grade! A grown-up! You were afraid to take off your backpack and put it down, in case you missed the bus while trying to put it on again. Bus number 761.

The last school picture I have of you is your school photo from sixth grade.

"I didn't like that school picture. The photographer made me twist my neck into this weird position."

But I liked it. You look so neat and sweet with your new haircut and the earrings I brought you from Thailand.

"And my favorite white shirt all buttoned up, the way *I* liked it."

*   *   *

Every time I see a schoolbus, my heart skips a beat. I dream about waiting for you to get off a schoolbus. Children get on and off, others wait in line. One or two girls even look a little bit like you in dim light or from a distance, slim and tall and wearing glasses. But you never come off any bus.

Gili's last school photo, sixth grade

It's never you. And once again I wake up crying. Every time I see a child getting off a bus, I hope it's you, and I cry when it's not. Every time I have to drive by one of your schools (and, believe me, I discovered many ways to avoid driving by) I feel that my heart is exploding from the pain. Before the schoolbus started picking you up, you used to stand right there, waiting for me to come. And there, I used to see you standing with a girl and chatting. You used to drop everything when you saw me coming. With a bright smile and a tired walk, you would approach me, insisting on carrying that bulky backpack of yours that probably weighed a ton.

"I was used to carrying it and you weren't. Therefore you shouldn't have tried because it would have hurt your back, Ima."

Your backpack became somewhat lighter in sixth grade. You were proud and relieved to have a locker.

"Like a grown-up."

You described some of your feelings about your first week of junior high school in your journal. You wrote: ". . . My first week of school wasn't the best, but it wasn't that horrible either." And you continued: ". . . Finally, I made it (survived) to my classroom. I got to the door and in, there were about seven kids in the classroom and four of them were looking at me awkwardly. I slowly crept in and greeted the teacher—when she called out my name as Jili and not Gili like the way it should be pronounced I answered, 'Here!' The reason why I did that is because I was very nervous and I forgot my name . . ."

I still laugh every time I read your journal! Your feelings did change, and again you did extremely well in every class.

During the last year, I noticed a rapid growth in you. It felt as if you were maturing in leaps, not developing at a gradual pace. Your intelligence sharpened. You were devouring information now, not just reading. Your intellectual curiosity became intense. You had always loved doing homework, but now you started spending many more hours doing extra homework—when asked to write one composition, you wrote three! When studying for an exam, you composed a sample test on your computer and tested yourself beforehand. You went to the library to read more about the topics being studied in class. The *Encyclopaedia Britannica* became your constant resource. You became a prolific writer of poetry, compositions, plays, and articles. I thought it was funny that you wrote your articles using the guidelines of the American Psychological Association.

"Why? I couldn't wait to become a psychologist, and I thought that I needed a lot of training."

Because of your training, your articles were better written than those of most of my graduate students at the university. You also used the dictionary a lot. The huge Oxford dictionary was still lying on the floor to the right of your desk, where you left it, until I moved to my new house. Remember how you would react whenever I asked Norm for the meaning of a word or for a spelling?

"I was hurt: Mommy, why didn't you ask me? I could have told you, too!"

Forgive me, my love. You were proud of your newly acquired knowledge. But at that time, especially when I was in my "me-no-speak-English" mode, I trusted Norm, the American, more than I trusted you. I am so sorry. But I did ask you at other times!

"Ima, Ima, remember how much we loved to talk about everything in the world?"

Do I remember—God, do I miss those conversations! Who criticizes plays with me? And books? And who updates me on popular music? Who "votes" with me on who would win the Miss America pageant. No matter what the candidates from Texas, Illinois, and Georgia looked like or sounded like, we always "voted" for them as finalists—loyalty was our rule! Who talks with me anymore about God? Whether He exists or not? And should one believe in Him or not?

"And a day before the accident, I decided that I believe in God. It made me feel peaceful."

Yes, I remember that. I wonder if it wasn't another premonition you had—making peace. And I remember the beginning of many other conversations, as your body began to mature.

"Mommy, I have these strange feelings in my body. Am I becoming a woman?" "How big will my tzi-tzi [breasts] be? At night in bed, I can almost hear my tzi-tzi growing," I remember you saying in laughter. "What is sexy?" "What is a teddy?" "Do I have to grow up?" "And what if I want to stay a child forever?" "Mommy," you said, "I am afraid to lose my sense of humor. Will I lose it when I grow up?" "I feel like a weird person sometimes. Does that mean that I'm becoming an adolescent?"

You'll grow up, Booba sheli, I used to reassure you. Don't you worry, Metuka sheli, you'll become a beautiful woman, I told you, loving, sensitive, and smart with a great sense of humor. How can you not?

"Sometimes you said, Ima, that I have no choice. I must have a great sense of humor because I have some Hungarian blood in me. We used to crack up laughing with that last statement. It pleased me that you acknowledged 'Daddy's side' in me. You did not dislike him that much, after all."

We could argue about that.

Other questions that you asked me were:

"Ima, will there ever be peace in Israel? Can people really live in peace with each other when they share so little and have so many differences?"

"Mommy sheli, can you and I do something for the homeless children? I feel so sad every time I see a homeless family in the streets."

"When I grow up I want to help children professionally, not as I do now. I want to be just like you. I'll be a professor and a psychologist and we'll work together, you and I."

"The children on the school bus that call me 'whitee'—aren't they racists?"

To this last I responded: Are you going to do anything about it?

And you answered, "Yes, I am going to tell them that they are making racist comments."

A week later I asked you what happened on the bus, and you told me that the children who called you names were so surprised when you told them that their comments were racist that they even forgot to argue with you. "But when they caught their breath," you said laughing, "they argued with me that because they were black, they could not be racists. I told them that being a racist has nothing to do with skin color. It has to do with attitudes toward other people that appear different than you are!"

You added that you didn't think that you convinced them, but it didn't matter because, "I believe it's true."

I believe it's true, too, my brave little Googi. I wish I had your guts.

One day, when you were still in fifth grade, you came home from a school trip to NASA. You were upset when you came home. Do you remember what upset you on that trip?

"Uh-huh, one of the teachers asked for volunteers to help her in carrying some heavy things to the bus. When I raised my hand to volunteer, she said to me, 'No, Gili, I want the boys to help me. It's heavy stuff.' I asked the teacher why can't girls carry heavy stuff? Are girls weaker than boys? The teacher ignored my questions. It really upset me. Don't you think, Mommy, that it was sexist?"

Yes, I think it was. And once again, I was so proud of you.

About a month before the accident, you crawled into my bed and, while cuddling with me, you whispered in my ear,

"Mommy, I am becoming more assertive," and with a smile added, "and I like it!"

School assignments in fifth grade on self-esteem helped in the development of your identity. I read passages in your notebooks where you described the things that you liked best about yourself. I agree that you were "loving, honest, creative, determined, and able to do most things."

"Ima, now you make me blush."

When you were asked to describe yourself, your likes, your hobbies and aspirations, you drew a profile that resembled yours and in it you drew symbols that described you best—a smiling face with a blackened tooth (we loved to blacken one tooth in our own mouths or on magazine photos of models) to represent your playfulness. A singing face symbolized your love for singing. A fishing rod—your new love, discovered thanks to Norm while vacationing on South Padre Island. A flower—your love for flowers, especially wildflowers. A strawberry—your favorite fruit. Shelly, your dog, wiggling her tail, right in the middle of your profile. Trees and a painter's palate—your love of painting. An open book—your love of reading. A caterpillar—your love of caterpillars and other animals, especially small and fragile ones, animals that needed "a Mommy." You liked to chew your pencils, so here it is—an unchewed pencil "before," and a chewed one "after." You also wrote the word *Humor* and drew a smiley face in the U—your sense of humor and creativity, as I see it. You wrote *Fossils*, another of your loves. Yale—the university you dreamed of attending to get a Ph.D. in psychology, and the University of Illinois and an academic cap to represent your hope to attend your parents' alma mater for your undergraduate studies. And of course, *Psychology*—your career goal.

"You engraved the 'book' and 'Shelly' on my gravestone."

Yes, I did. I thought that they expressed your aspirations and your likes. Your attachment to your dog expressed you, as do the other engravings—those of an open book, your sculpture of our hands holding a golden heart, and the Chanukah menorah with the eighth candle missing.

Gili's "profile"

"Yes, I even know what you had in mind: If children visited my grave, it would not be a frightening place."

Yes, that too, but also that it tells a story about you. I wanted the stone to "tell" a meaningful (although limited) story about you, and I wanted the visitor to "see" beyond the stone, beyond your name and the two dates—of your birth and death.

In another "self-portrait" your descriptions of self, likes, and aspirations were more abstract: In this painting, which now dominates my study wall, you drew a hand, your hand erupting from the ground. You described it to me as symbolizing your "trying to reach out and reach up." You drew the moon that fascinated you at the time, a wildflower, a painter's brush, a chewed-up pencil, and an open book with a marker—all planted and erupting or perhaps growing from the ground. I wonder—was it another premonition-type painting? This painting, which you made a month before the accident, still gives me the chills.

Although you took your school assignments very seriously, you did not take yourself that way. Very often you used humor in your "serious" home-

Gili's headstone and gravestone—before Norm's death

Another "self-portrait" with Gili's hand "reaching out and up"

work. One of the first compositions that you wrote in sixth grade is a typical example:

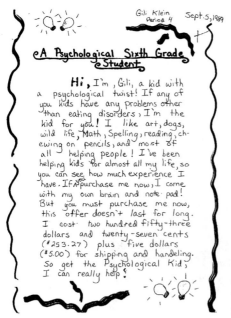

A humoristic description of a "psychologically oriented" sixth grader

I loved the "Hi, I'm Gili, a kid with a psychological twist!" You could always make me laugh and cry. God! Why?!

You loved to make fashion sketches. One of them was of your prom dress. At least in your fantasy, my love, you went to your prom . . .

"I liked that outfit. Didn't you, Mom?"

Yes, I did. I would have been happy to make it for you. I can almost see you wearing it.

In *Writing a Description*, you described how an artist should paint laughter! Liz, a former friend, followed your instructions—she and another artist painted and framed your composition. I wish you could see it.

> I would have wanted the artist to paint me a picture of what they think is laughter. The artist would blend a variety of bright, dull, and dark colors. The artist would shape this blend of colors in a large circle. They would start the circle using a peacock blue to show sadness, a pearl blue to show the mixed feeling of being happy and sad, and a navy blue to symbolize morose feelings in laughter. Next to these sad feelings would be a pitch dark black space to symbolize

One of many fashion drawings by Gili—her dream for a prom outfit hatefulness and jealousy. After that there would be a grey space to show dullness in the laughter and a white space to show fakeness in laughter. Next to the white space, there would be a rouje red space to symbolize love, a plain orange to show happiness, a bright like full of excitement orange to symbolize the humor, and a peach space to represent affection. After that, there would be a sunny yellow to represent excitement, a gold to symbolize pride, a pale faded green to show friendship, a lavender to symbolize sensitivity, and a dark gloomy purple to symbolize fear and nervousness. That would have been the painting I would have liked the artist to have painted. After the artist would have finished painting the painting, they would have bordered it in a wooden border made out of pine and had a lily, the size of three fingers put together, carved into each of the four rounded corners of the border.

"Mommy, don't forget Yonaleh and Beenee."

Oh yes, the mourning doves that you rescued from the bad weather and from the black cat. You put them in our atrium, fed them, and cried when they disappeared one day. We had to reassure you that nothing bad happened to them, that because of you they were strong enough to fly away and look for their mother.

After you died, for the last 8 years, at least once a day, a mourning dove has appeared, cooing sadly. Strange. Is she also looking for you, or is she carrying a message from you? I didn't see her or hear her for a while. I began to wonder if she had a "timetable" for mourning or mourners, but then she returned.

In your typical scientific-artistic manner, you observed Beenee's and Yonaleh's behavior and drew a humorous cartoon of them. Here they are—Beenee, the aggressive one, and Yonaleh, the gentle one. That picture, to me, symbolizes life—conflicts, polarities in character and in behavior. So whenever I feel torn inside by conflicting emotions, whenever I feel a need to be reassured by you that the way I feel is OK, I kiss that picture. I feel touched then by you.

"One of my dreams was to write children's books. Did I tell you?"

No, but I suspected it, because you cared so deeply about children and you loved to write. Maybe one day I will fulfill your dream. I would like to include some of your stories in a children's book.

You wrote several poems about the moon. It seems to me that at times you were both frightened and fascinated by that celestial body of light: The silvery-bluish beam that flooded your room, on a full-moon night, transformed it and triggered your imagination. I can see you lying in the dark, the covers over your head with only a "tunnel" made for your nose to

The mourning doves: Beenee and Yonaleh

breathe, your little heart palpitating in excitement. You tried to extend the day as much as you could, to push the night away, but there was no escape: You had to face your fears by yourself—and you did.

November 15, 1988   Gili Klein

THE MOON

The moon is round, the moon is bold.
    As it shines through the night,
it looks as bright as it looks down at me,
    it says, "My dear young fellow, you look
so mellow, what ever could be wrong?"
    so I answer,
"My dear and lovely moon, I have just
    seen "Platoon" and it really does
scare me!"
    "Oh, my dear young fellow,
you should not be so mellow just because
    you have seen Platoon,
for life is a movie, you are the main
    character and have the main part,
sometimes you get scared and sometimes not,
    so don't be worried if one
movie scares you."
    "Oh, I shall not." says I,

and left the moon with a silent cry.
      And this is the story of the
moon and I.

by Gili Klein

   You coped with day-to-day worries by discussing them with me and
with your close friends. But you also expressed yourself through your artistic work—writing, painting, sculpting, sewing, and any other media that
you came across. On March 21, 1989, you drew this picture. This one really
scared me when I first saw it. But when you described to me what you had
tried to express, I was once again amazed at how you deal with your anxieties, at your optimism and incredible zest for life.
   I can still see your earnest expression when you said, "This is a person
who has a very dreary life and tries to stop it—and happiness flows in."
   Sometimes you said that you didn't want to grow old. At other times
you said that you wanted to grow up, but you also wanted us to stay together and live forever. In the cartoon booklet called "Gili Growing Old,"
which you devoted to "Mommy and Normi," your dedication, on the second page of the booklet, still makes me choke. You described yourself

A drawing of emotions: anxiety and hope

aging. You expressed your dreams of becoming a professor at age 25; then, realizing that it might sound immodest, you erased it. And you wrote a wish—"I will live to be 96, 97, 99,—100, and longer. I hope you both will also live to be older than 100."

I hope not (not me), my love. I cannot and I do not want to live that long without you! It has been too long already.

You knew how to love. You knew how to express love. You knew how to give and you loved to give. I remember our first Rosh Hashanah with Norm. Norm and I got into an argument about going to services at the synagogue. We sat down for dinner that night, very upset. You asked us, trying to read our facial expressions, "What's going on?" I responded that it was hard for me to talk about it now. Do you remember what you said to us?

"Yes, I remember. I said 'Ima, I think that we are not honest with each other. We don't say how we feel. Only I am open.'"

That was another lesson for us. You were my guide then. You are my guide now.

Even when you got angry at times, or when we were angry at you (for staying up late until past your bedtime; chatting on the phone "forever"; remembering at the last minute, right before closing hour, that you "must" have some thing or another for school for the next day—God! Let me trade my life for another minute of these "annoyances"), your typical reaction was to go to your room, close yourself in your bathroom, and talk out-loud your frustrations with us. This would usually take no more than half an hour; you would then come out of your room with open arms, teary eyes, a long face, and an "upside-down smily" pout. You looked very, very sad.

You would then say, "Mommy, I need a hug. I want us to talk about what happened. I don't want to hurt your feelings, but I also don't want you and Norm to hurt mine."

You took risks, my love. And that was another lesson of loving.

To watch you prepare a gift was also a lesson in love. The attention you paid to every detail: What did the person for whom you made the gift like? What would please him or her? Would your gift express exactly what your feelings were? You found time to give your gifts, and you did not need special occasions for giving. You never expected anything in return. In fact, you used to say that you had too much already. And you meant not just earthly possessions.

Here is the miniature sculpture that you made for Norm and me for our first anniversary: The hands are in a light blue color and the heart is in yellow-gold.

Gili Growing
Old

illustrated by: Gili Klein

by: Gili Klein

"Gili growing old"

Dedicated to my wonderful
mommy and daddy, Norm and Henya
Kagan. My parents are so,
I don't know how to write
it, they are what words can
not describe! I love you
more than anybody in the
whole wide world!

Published on March 13, 1989
Made when author was ten years old.

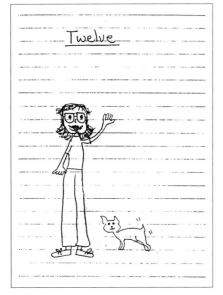

Twelve

Forty-Two

Sixty-Five

Ninety-Five

I will live to be 96, 97, 98, 99, 100, and longer. I hope you both will also live to be older than 100.

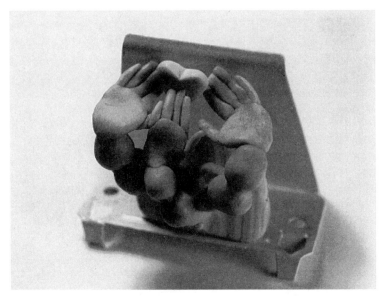

Gili's gift for our first wedding anniversary: a miniature sculpture of our hands holding a golden heart

You described your gift with these words: "This sculpture represents our hands and us as a family. We always hold on and stay together. We're always strong, and when we're not strong at certain moments we always help each other. We always reach for the best things in life, but sometimes we don't get them. That is why the color of our hands are blue. But sometimes we do get them and that's why the blue is a very light color. But either way our hearts will always be bright, shining, colorful, and full of love!" You drew the exclamation mark in a heart shape, and you signed:

"By Gili Klein

11 years old 8/28/89."

You did not take any relationship for granted. You kept reminding us how precious our time together was. How important we were to you. How much you loved us, and how crucial loving is. You had two typical gestures that still bring tears to my eyes. One was putting your hand on my shoulder very lightly as we were driving. I then used to kiss your hand—we reassured each other. The other, whenever I did something for you that you especially appreciated or when you didn't expect it, was that your huge eyes would get teary and you would lift my hand so very gently to your lips and kiss it. I had never felt so loved in my entire life. I never knew anybody like you. How, God, can I go on living without my life?

On every wall or door, in every corner or drawer in the house, you left pictures and notes of love. The notes, Gili, are slowly fading away—loosing their colors and form. But your love will never fade away. And that, Yalda sheli, was the greatest lesson that you taught me.

"Mommy, did you find the love notes that I left for you under the 'Elephant' trunk? And in the little basket with the dry baby-azalea? And what about the 'Love' tree that I made for you and Norm. Do you still have them?"

Yes, my Giligooli. I found them, and I cherish them. I read the notes very often, holding them with trembling hands and a crying heart. They are so delicate, and you are not around to make new ones.

*   *   *

You loved to travel—visiting friends, old and new places. In the year and 4 months that we lived in Houston, we traveled several times out of state and within the state. One of the trips we took was to see the famous wildflowers of Texas. You immersed yourself in that spread-out carpet of vibrant colors—purple-blue, red-orange, yellow, pink, maroon, and white. All surrounded by lush green. Your artist's eye couldn't have enough. You skipped and rolled, and ran and laughed, as if you were about to explode from happiness. You were drunk on all that beauty.

We drove to San Antonio and visited all the important tourists' sights. At the Alamo a veil of sadness covered your face when you heard about the men who were killed right where we were standing. At Sea World, you wanted us to take a picture of you lying on the map of Illinois. Urbana wasn't on the map, so you pointed at Champaign—close enough.

"Ima, I loved the trip on the boat that you and I took in New Orleans. I didn't like, though, the drunk people in the streets and the strip joints in the French Quarter."

Your curiosity about sex was budding, but you were also appalled and embarrassed to see how women exploit themselves—my little feminist. Since our first days in the States, which started in a small motel in Urbana, Illinois, one of your greatest joys was to stay in a hotel. So here we are in New Orleans, in front of the hotel. God, can you give me that time back?

"Mommy, don't cry. Remember how I helped you in your presentation at that conference in Washington?"

Do I remember—and how can I not cry? You behaved like a professional—you amazed everybody by the interest you showed and the smart questions you asked the presenters. I was shocked to see you, my shy kiddo, walking around the presentation hall, introducing herself to people. Chatting and asking professional questions, collecting presentation papers.

"I read them all."

The three of us in New Orleans

I saw that. And you answered questions about the research paper that I presented! Unbelievable. You were meant to be a scientist—a psychologist, so we thought.

You loved Washington—the museums, the monuments; although after walking The Mall for the third time in a week, we were both ready to go back to driving in a car and never to walk in a city again.

I think that I know which vacation was the best you ever had . . .

"The week on South Padre Island. I was only sorry that Guy didn't want to join us. But I was happy anyway!"

And we were happy, too, in spite of the hurt. We ran on the white sand beaches, we had deep discussions with seagulls, and most important of all—you discovered a real talent for catching fish. You were a born fisherwoman!

Norm, who taught you the new skill (one morning, before 6:00 in the morning—when God was still asleep), was amazed to see with what ease you surpassed him and the other "professional" fishermen in catching fish. You caught exactly 15 fish the first time you tried fishing! I don't remember your eating any of these fish, but I remember your throwing some of them back to sea. I guess, after you name a fish, it's hard to eat it.

Gili, the fisherwoman, talking to the seagulls

On August 25, 1989, we celebrated your eleventh birthday.
"My last birthday."
Are you crying, my love, or is it my heart?
You invited a few of your best friends from fifth grade to a swimming-pool party. My thoughts wander to other happy times you and I had in that pool. Do you remember how you insisted on carrying me around in the pool in your arms? "Like a cupcake," you said, laughing. When you were less than a year old, I had carried you the same way in another pool, in Ashkelon—you were my cupcake than—I was yours now—imprisoned in your thin but strong arms. I loved it. I still choke up when going by the pool. I can see you diving into the deep end and calling to me, "Ima, look, look what I can do!" while I held my breath until you surfaced. You used to laugh at my fear of deep water, and you promised to teach me to swim in deep water so I could overcome my fear. Where are you, my teacher?
"Every day of the week before my birthday you gave me a different present. I told you, Mommy, that it's too much, but I really liked the little surprises under my pillow. You'd never done it before. Why did you do it that time, Ima?"

I cannot explain, Yalda sheli. I just felt an urgent need to shower you with gifts. I kept hearing a nagging whisper in my head—"as if there is no tomorrow." Was it a premonition? I wanted every moment of your birthday to be memorable. My heart expanded in joy when I heard the laughter, the giggles, and the water splashing coming from the pool. For a few hours we transformed the entire pool area in our neighborhood into a party, with decorations, candles, and your favorite cake—my version of a strawberry shortcake. But when we sang "Happy birthday, dear Gili—Happy birthday to you" I choked, and you looked sad. Why were you sad, Tooki sheli?

"I felt sad, Mommy, because it was another separation. I wasn't 11 anymore; I started 12. I was growing up so fast, it scared me. I liked being a kid. I wasn't sure about being an adolescent. And I had to say goodbye again to my old friends."

Or did you and I have a premonition that day, that we were approaching a final separation? What was it that day that made us feel so sad, I wonder. When Norm suggested that we should "leave something for next year," I looked at him, uncomprehending: Next year? "We have only now!" That voice kept pounding in my ears—"We have only now."

*   *   *

Just before Thanksgiving, exactly one month before the car crash, I felt, for the first time in my adult life, a pressing urge to be comforted by my own mother. I could not explain what overcame me. I just needed to go to Israel and visit my mother and sister.

You begged me, "Please, Mommy, take me with you. I miss Savta Aimi. I haven't seen my family since I was 7."

I had to refuse. There was still a real threat: The American custody order didn't hold in Israel. Forgive me, my love. I could not take the risk that either you or I might be held in the country against our will.

So I left with a heavy heart and you stayed with Norm. You had a good time together—going to a circus that visited Houston, cooking the Thanksgiving dinner, and saving some for me.

Our last Passover was a happy one. We had guests at the Seder.

"And you gave me my first bra."

I can hear you giggle. I remember you trying it on later that night, embarrassed but pleased that I thought you were old enough to wear a bra.

You asked me with a shy smile, "Ima, do you think that I really need a training bra?"

No, Tooki sheli, I said. Whatever you are growing there does not need training, but you wanted to feel like a grown-up girl, and grown-up girls wear bras. As we hugged in the middle of your room, we were mother and daughter embraced in womanhood.

Gili helping in preparations of her last
Thanksgiving dinner

Then came your very last Chanukah. Your most beloved holiday—
candle lighting, singing, playing special games, festive dinners for eight
nights. Even Nature came forward for you that Chanukah. You loved snow,
so it snowed just for you. We felt happy and close to each other.

We planned to celebrate your Bat-Mitzvah in Israel. Nevertheless, your
father came to Houston to meet his lawyer and to visit you. And on your
way back from visiting with him, the killer awaited you at the entrance to
our home—30 feet away from the Chanukah dinner table, 30 feet away from
life. Why did he have to come?

During that last week of your life, you did not feel well. You were
haunted by nightmares of a man chasing you and trying to kill you. You
told me, still shaking, "I fell down off my bike, dead." And then you asked
me, "Mommy, what is a head injury?" When I told you what it meant, you
said in such a quiet voice that ran a chill through my body, "I hope that I'll
never have a head injury." Was it another premonition?

A day before the car crash, you developed a fever. You came into my
bed that morning and asked me if you could stay in bed with me and
not go to visit your father that day. We hugged and kissed, but Norm took
you anyway because we were supposed to deliver you to your father
every day of his visit to Houston. I wish I had kept you in my arms
forever.

Snow in Houston—Gili's last Chanukah

Later that night, just before your bedtime, I saw you for a brief moment. You were undressed, on your way to take a shower. I felt a sudden urge to take you in my arms. I rushed over to you and we clung to each other in a long hug. I told you that "I love you more than life itself," and you responded while kissing me, "and I love you Mommy, more than life." You added, "and I will love you forever and ever." Me too, my child, me too.

All that time I felt, no, heard a voice saying, "As if it's the last time." It scared me—hugging you as if it's the last time? What did it mean?

And what did you mean the night before when you asked me, "Mommy, what will you do *when* I die?"

My blood chilled in my veins—When you die? Don't talk like that, I begged you. I have no life without you. I'll die.

With tears in your eyes, you hugged me and said, "No, Mommy, I don't want you to die. Don't be afraid—I'll live forever. Please promise me that you'll also live forever." So we promised each other to live and love forever.

Friday morning, December 29, 1989, the day of the accident, I woke up covered with cold sweat. I heard you coming to my bedroom door. I knew that you wanted to give me a goodbye kiss before leaving with Norm to see your father in his hotel. I heard you approaching the door, and then you stopped. Instead of coming into my room, I heard Norm asking you not to wake me up and urging you to come because it was getting late. To my dismay, you walked away. I ran after you. I had to see you. But you left. I could hear Norm's car pulling away. I felt crushed. Why? The rest of the day I felt as if my heart was about to burst out of my body, as if I was held together only by my skin. I was shaking. I had heart palpitations and I felt extremely anxious, as if something awful was about to happen. Why? I had never felt like that in my entire life.

You promised to call me at noon.

You said, "I miss you when I'm away, and I want to tell you that I love you." So you asked me, "please, Ima, be at home at 12:30."

I was, my love, but we missed each other by only 5 minutes—an eternity. You called at 12:25, and I was left with a recording of your sweet voice, never to be heard again—not in this world anyway.

I spent the rest of the day, after the missed phone call, "climbing the walls." I kept telling Norm that I didn't know what was happening to me, but I felt that something horrible was going to happen. Norm could not calm me down. When he left for his office, I started cooking all your favorite dishes. I drew designs for earrings for you. I wanted to discuss the designs with you and have the earrings with your favorite peridots (your birth stone) made for your twelfth (your Bat-Mitzvah) birthday. While drawing and loading up the kitchen table with dishes, my hands were trembling, my heart palpitating, cold sweat sending shivers along my back, and a nagging voiceless thought kept saying—"As if you can hold her here forever—magical thinking—magical thinking . . ."

Finally, there was nothing left to put on the table. I even put all nine candles in the Menorah, to be lit by you in a few moments. I sat down, glued to my chair, counting the crawling minutes and my racing heartbeats. Suddenly, it all happened at once—a car's brakes screeching—a horrifying crashing sound of metal on metal—a bang on our front door—and a scream "Henya!" Later, Norm swore that he never called me. Who called then? Bewildered, I ran to the door. Shelly was barking violently. Nobody was at the door. Who called my name? The telephone rang—a man's voice, "There was an accident." I hung up the phone—"What does he mean? What accident? No it cannot happen. Norm just went to pick you up from your father's hotel. You are right here, down the street—it's not you—it's a mistake . . ." The telephone rang again—a woman's voice, "There was an accident. Here. Your husband is fine."

"Where is my daughter?!" I screamed. "How is my child?"

"She is wounded. She is outside your house . . ."

I ran, I flew, I didn't hear the rest. In an instant, I saw you lying on the ground, Norm covered with blood. The killing driver standing at a distance. The two cars totaled. Everything slowed down. From then on, every minute would be recorded in slow motion. Time would be measured by how much life was left in you—as if we were put into a sand clock. I heard myself screaming, "Gili!" I saw your delicate face lying in a growing pool of blood. A small stream of blood coming out of your right ear. Your blood, your life, my love, running into the ground—you tried to roll your eyes when you heard my voice. I knew I shouldn't touch you—even the slightest move was dangerous. You were not breathing. You were in a coma! It stopped drizzling. The ambulance's siren stopped. And a voiceless thought whispered in my brain—"She does not belong to you." God! Shut up!

Gili, what happened, Yalda sheli? Please tell me what happened to you? As if in a dream, I can hear you in my mind's ear. Your voice so soft and slow:

"Mommy, the last that I remember was that I sat buckled up in the backseat, as usual. I was telling Norm what I did with Daddy today. The last thing I said was, 'I had fun today at the IMAX theater and at the Museum of Natural Science, and I have a little bit of a headache from watching the IMAX, but it's OK.' I hardly finished saying it when from the corner of my eye I saw a light coming at me from the dark. It was a car zooming at us at a crazy speed. 'Mommy!' I screamed, but no voice came out. I could hear the screeching sound of breaks, metal crashing, glass shattering. I felt being torn off my seat and thrown in and out of the car window. Then the whole world exploded in my head.

"The next thing I knew, I was floating in the air. It was dark. I didn't feel any pain, but I was scared. I felt panic. What was happening? How come I'm lying down there on the ground but I'm up here? I could see that my eyes were closed, blood was running out of my right ear, and I couldn't move. People were standing around me. Then, out of the darkness I heard your voice, Mommy. You screamed to me, 'Gili! Al tefachadi! Mummily, zot Ima, al tefachadi! Ani itach yalda sheli!' (Gili! Don't be afraid! Mummily, it's Mom, don't be afraid! I'm with you my child!). I could hear you very well. I tried to talk to you. I wanted to ask you what had happened to me. Was Norm hurt? But again, no voice came out. I tried to move my legs and hands, but they didn't respond to me. I couldn't breathe. This really scared me. It was the first time that I was afraid that I was dead! Then I felt that I could roll my eyes. You saw it! I was less scared. I was not all alone in the dark. 'I don't want to die! Please God, I don't want to die!' I could hear myself pleading and crying. I was not ready to die yet. I loved my life. Because I loved you more than I loved anybody in the whole wide world, I didn't want to leave you, Ima.

"In the hospital, the doctors tried to save me. They operated on my injured brain. For five days I was in a coma. I felt as if I was floating in and out of my body. I was more confused than in pain. It was very frustrating and sometimes frightening to hear you crying or talking to me, because I could not talk or move or breathe. I could feel you touching me. I even knew that you flew in my brother to be with me. I could hear and feel all of you. I could see you with my closed eyes. Don't ask me how, I just could. I tried to roll my eyes, to let you know that I heard you. I squeezed your hand, Mommy, and Daddy's and my brother's and Norm's. I didn't want to let go of your hand. I was afraid to be alone in the dark. But I already knew that I wasn't coming back to you. You, my Mommile, knew that, too. For you, Ima, I tried to hold on to what was left of my life as long as I could.

"On the fifth day, around 4:00 in the afternoon, I was finally ready to leave. The doctor came out and said, 'Gili is braindead!' I was horrified. My brain is dead? What does it mean? How is it possible that the brain that I was so proud of is dead! You were very pale and sad when you came into my room. You looked as if you were dead, not me. You took me in your arms very slowly and gently. You touched me with the tips of your fingers, as you used to do when I pretended to be asleep in my room. You touched me all over with your lips, as if you were trying to imprint every bump of my skin through your lips, into your brain and heart. I heard you then whispering to me, in the saddest voice that I've ever heard in my life, 'Lechi yalda sheli im at ayefa. Ze besedr iti. Al tefachadi lalechet. Ani ohevet otach leolam vaed.' (Go, my child, if you are tired. It's OK with me. Don't be afraid to go. I love you forever and ever.)

"The doctor asked if you would like to donate my organs. My organs! I could not believe it. It took me a long moment to understand—I don't need my body anymore. So why not help somebody to live. I was relieved to hear you answering the doctor, 'Gili had a good heart. You may take her heart. She would have liked that.' And I did. It did not scare me at all. I was a little bit curious—so many new things were happening to me. So when the crying and praying and pleading didn't help—I left. It surprised me, how peaceful I felt—sad but not scared. I felt as if I was about to go on a long trip, the first time in my life by myself. I was sad to go alone and leave everybody and everything I loved and knew behind me. But I was also excited. I love adventures.

"I knew that you, Ima, would mourn for me for the rest of your life. I can see the heart-shaped garden you planted on the spot where I was thrown out of Norm's car. 'Gili Klein's Garden' says the sign you put there. I knew that you would never stop missing me, and that I would always miss you. I wished that I could hug you and give you a big smoochy kiss and tell you that everything was going to be OK, but I couldn't. We had been together, I thought, only 11 years, 4 months, and 5 days. But I wouldn't change a thing; in spite of the hurt and pain, we loved each other with all our hearts. I knew, don't ask me how, I just knew, that you were going to be with me again when it's your time to pass over to the Next World. I knew that I would be with you in spirit all the time even if you could see me, hear me, or feel me only in your mind and heart. I am real as you are real. Now, I'm fine. All is well. Don't cry, Mommy, please don't cry."

A memorial to Gili–the heart-shaped garden

INTERLUDE

"Between the Worlds"

"Yitgadal veitkadash shmei raba, bealma divra chirutei. . . ." Magnified and sanctified be the name of God throughout the world which He hath created according to His will. . . .

—Mourner's Kaddish

I recited this prayer, in Aramaic, twice a day for the whole first year, and then on special holidays and on the Yahrzeit, the anniversary of the day of the death. The Kaddish has become my mantra. The words, the rhythm, transcend me to another sphere. Sharp pain still cuts through my chest when I say it—it means that you are dead! The Kaddish is said for the dead, in honor of and for the exaltation of the soul. My daughter, in honor of you I will continue reciting the Kaddish for the rest of my life. As I did every day for the first year, I will continue lighting a special candle for you every Friday night when I light the Shabbat candles. It is said in the Chassidut (Jewish mysticism) that a single candle is sufficient to light up a vast darkness. You and I were always looking for symbols. You were my light in darkness. The candle light symbolizes the light that you brought into this world while alive and continue to bring into the Next World. Now I light a second candle for Norm, and I recite another Kaddish for him, too.

"Mommy, to me the candlelight symbolized the happiness of being together—you and I surrounded by light. I saw the melting of the candle as the gradual disappearance of sadness and the increase of light flowing into our lives."

Yes, my sweetheart, I remember very well the picture you gave me of you and I inside candlelight. It hangs on the wall in front of me.

You wrote along the side of your drawing:

This is me laying in my bed and my mom reading me a story in the light. There is yellow light around me and my mom because yellow is a color of happiness and me and my mom are happy. The blue candle is melting because blue is a color of sadness and it's melting

79

1/11/89

Gili's drawing and description of me and her
inside the light of a candle

away, in other words the sadness is melting away. And as you can
see the happiness (light) is bigger so when the candle (sadness) melts
the sadness dies and the happiness gets bigger.

As I look at a picture of you, I pretend to hold your hand while praying, or crying, or talking to you. Then I kiss your forehead, your heart, your
hands—again and again, as I did on your deathbed. *Deathbed!* Yours! God
in Heaven! I looked at you, lying there as if you were asleep. Your small
face surrounded by a big bandage. Your beautiful cascading hair, shaved
underneath the bandage. A tube coming out of your thin chest. Your delicate skin punctured right under your budding breast. Your full lips sucking on a large tube. You were warm to the touch and rosy. And the doctor
told me that it was time to say "goodbye," that you were braindead. The
scream that started in my head, in my inner ear, and in the essence of my
soul will last until the end of time.

At about 4:30 in the afternoon, on a bitterly cold Wednesday, I was finally allowed to take you in my arms. I held you and kissed you so gently,
whispering over and over in your ear: "Lechi Yalda sheli im at ayefa" (Go,
my child, if you are tired). And added: "I'll be fine." Then, suddenly, I *felt*
your soul leaving your body. I cannot explain it. Until that moment, the
concept of survival of the soul was not part of my philosophy. Until that
moment I was not ready to contemplate the idea that there is a God; but I

had no specific need to ponder or to develop a firm belief in Him. I had not paid special attention to writings that described the soul's departure from the body, its floating above it or close to the ceiling. However, intuitively, I looked up to the left corner of the ceiling, right above your bed. For an unknown reason, I had a distinct feeling that you were there, floating and looking at me. I also had the feeling that you could hear me, so I kept talking to you.

"You said to me, that I may leave you if I choose so. That I shouldn't be afraid because a wonderful trip is awaiting me. You asked me to wait for you when it's your time to come, and you asked me to visit you if I can. And all that time you kept telling me that you loved me more than life and I should not be scared."

Where did my words come from? I wonder. They were not typical of my thinking at that time; nevertheless they felt right. I acknowledged the fact that I felt your soul leaving your body at a particular moment, and I experienced you in the room afterwards. Hearing myself saying these words to you almost in detachment, and at the same time being more attached to myself and to Life than ever before, was the turning point in my worldview. I felt as though a veil was lifted and for a brief moment I was given the privilege to glance at Greatness. The doctor's soft voice, asking my permission to donate your organs (*your organs!*), awakened me from a deep dream—or should I say, "nightmare"? After only a brief discussion with your father, brother, and Norm, they left the decision to me. I knew what you would have wanted if we only had had a chance to talk about organ donation. You always gave so generously to others. There was no way that you would have refused an opportunity to save another's life by your giving, I thought. I told the doctor: "Gili had a good heart. Take her heart. She would have liked that." (I had to talk about you immediately in the *past* tense. No time to adjust). And your heart was harvested. And it saved another's life.

"I knew, Mommy. I would have made the same decision about you, Ima."

A few days later, when Shiva started, the house was completely transformed. Many people came to pray and to pay their respects. All the mirrors in the house were covered, according to Jewish tradition. And a seven-day candle was lit. From the very first moments of Shiva, again I felt your presence very strongly. But more than that, I could feel that you were bewildered by your new condition and by the happenings in our house. You and I were not accustomed to the Orthodox tradition. You had never been in a house of mourners. All of this was new and frightening. Once again, from a source unknown to me, out came the following words: "Al tefachadi Yalda sheli . . . (don't be afraid my child), this is what a house of mourners looks like. People have gathered in your honor to say Kaddish, a special prayer said for the elevation of your soul. Just let the prayer soothe you. Let the candle light up your way. Let your soul continue to grow and develop and to lighten up this world as well as the Other World. Don't be scared, my love" (all said in Hebrew).

"Ima, I remember that you walked around the house as if you were giving me a guided tour, and so we walked, our hands clinging to each other, mother and daughter, taking the saddest walk of our lives. I can still hear your voice, very low and sad, the saddest I ever heard, telling me that the mirrors were covered because at the time of mourning we should focus our attention inward and not be distracted by our vanity as reflected in the mirror. Mommy, how did you know all that?"

I did not. These and the other words just came to my mind. I had never heard nor read them before. And I am not even sure that this was the correct explanation. It just felt right at that moment. And I felt that you calmed down somewhat. Although for what felt like a long time, I felt you were bouncing from wall to wall and from room to room in confusion and terror. I could hear you pleading, begging in a terrified voice: "Ima, ma kore iti?" (Mom, what is happening to me?) I told you that you could come and visit us whenever you wished. You might want to stay in your room or play with your dog, Shelly, but eventually you would need to continue your trip alone. I called it "tiyul" (trip or journey), remember?

"Yes, Ima. And you also said that it would be the first time that I had gone on a 'tiyul' by myself, but it would be OK. Your father, the grandpa I had never known, and other relatives whom I had never met, would be with me. And they were. How did you know that?"

I did not.

In the beginning, I screamed to God in resentment—"Why?" Then I asked Him for new understanding and for comfort. Finally, I turned into myself for an inner search. I realized that mourning is a journey taken in solitude. In my despair and devastation, I asked you: "Mommile, help me! I don't want to live without you! But if I'm doomed to live, tell me how to live."

You gave me your answer during Shiva. I heard you saying to me in a very soft voice in Hebrew: "Ima, al tichassi" (Mother, don't be angry). I trust your help and I listen to you. I always did, Mommile. At the time I felt that you were directing me toward a mission: How to take care of myself, how to achieve a deeper understanding of grief, and, ultimately, how to help others who suffered a devastating loss.

As long as I live, I will continue praying to God for your soul to grow and to develop and for you to do well for yourself and for others. When I talk to you, I ask you to continue bringing light into your life and into ours.

I can rarely say anything then. I just cry to you as I look at your picture, this picture that Norm took on your last Thanksgiving day. This picture will always have a central place wherever I live.

In my mind I can hear you saying, "I remember. I came down to the kitchen in my nightgown, and I opened Mommy's new 'lazy chair.' Shelly jumped on my lap, and I was surprised because Shelly never liked to sit on my lap. I asked Norm to take a picture of us. Even Norm was surprised to see Shelly curled up in my lap. I know, Ima. You would say that both Shelly and I had a premonition, that this was the last time that she would sit on my lap. When the picture was developed I named it 'Mommy and Baby.' I liked it because I could see Shelly's eyes. Now, they look sad to me. So maybe there is something in that 'premonition' idea."

PREMONITIONS

Let's talk about premonitions a little bit more. In retrospect, I can identify a series of events that gave me the chills even at the time they occurred. Let me just mention a few, and we'll wonder about their meaning together.

"Remember, Mommy? Just a month before the accident, I stayed up one night to write a composition called *The Street*."

Yes, I remember. You showed it to me. "What do you think, Ima; would my English teacher like it?" You asked me eagerly. I can still see your smile

Gili with Shelly on her lap—"Mommy and baby"

when I told you that she would love it. "But why these images of death?"
I asked you, my voice disclosing a tremble. You answered and shrugged
your shoulders: "This is how I felt. I cannot explain why."

The Street

A cold, meanhearted, fateless feeling
rushes through your blood as you rush
across it. A hard black gravel—stoned floor
pounds on your feet as you stomp on it.
Crystalline lights with joyous colors flash
and flicker as you stare at them.
Mechanical death machines zooming
with fateless speed go by you as you
try to intervene between them. As
you try to rush across it you see a
peaceful, silent, clearance at the
other side. You hope you will make it
across, but of course it is well known
that you are taking a great chance
with life across this rectangular
line of horror, the street.
Gili Klein
11/8/89

Several days later, while doing your homework in Language, you were
supposed to describe a situation and then make a distinction among
thoughts, feelings, and actions that resulted from that situation. From all
the examples you could have chosen, you had a need to give this one:

Situation: You were walking down the street with your friend, suddenly
they get knocked down by a car. They start to cry because their body
hurts. You ask them if they can get up, but they can't and nobody around
you is paying attention.
Thoughts: I am in trouble. Maybe I should scream for help. Maybe I leave
her, no I shouldn't.
Feelings: I'm scared, frightened. My anxiety level is high. I'm nervous.
Actions: I screamed for help.

Is this how you felt a month and two days later when you were the one
to be "knocked down" by the car?
On your last day of school, just before Christmas break, your art teacher

told me (she was still shaking her head in disbelief) that you came over to her, shook her hand, and told her, "It was nice meeting you, Ms. Dolores, thank you." Your teacher told me that she felt chills when you said that. She asked you then, "Why, Gili, aren't you coming back after Christmas? Are you going to visit your family in Israel?"

She did not remember your answer. She had the impression that you mumbled something. A few days earlier, you had made your teacher feel "strange," as she said, when you showed her your last painting—a class project on describing oneself. You were planning to complete it, but you never did. Not on this earth.

In this large painting, you drew two hands. The left one is blue and the right one is skin color. The hands are trying to touch each other, but a zig-zagged line separates them. Surrounding the hands are planets and erupting ground with grass growing on top. It may look like a fresh gravesite from underneath the ground, or a scene somewhere in space.

"Ms. Dolores asked me what that painting meant, and I said: The line between the hands separates between the worlds. The blue hand symbol-izes the unknown, weird space or world—sort of lost in space."

What did you mean, my love, by "the worlds" and "lost in space"? Where did these images and concepts come from? Why then and never before? And why did you feel that these were the images to describe yourself?

Gili's unfinished drawing of "the hands across the worlds"

How can I explain the following poem you left for me one day during this last year, in which you wrote about yourself,

> She went one day in an old
> fashion way,
> And never came back, poor
> old Gili!

During the last year and 4 months, Gili, you wrote, drew, and initiated conversations with me about topics surrounding death—yours and mine, believing in God, making peace with people, ghosts, head injuries and car accidents, to mention a few.

"I remember, I sensed I made you feel uncomfortable and even frightened whenever I brought these topics up."

And when I asked you why these issues were bothering you and what was going on, you used to shrug and say, "I don't know, Mommy. I don't mean to scare you but I have these weird feelings." When I asked you if you felt anxious about something, you answered, "No. Not especially."

Then you woke up one night, screaming.

When you were safe in my arms, you told me: "Ima, this man was chasing me. He was trying to kill me." When I asked you if he succeeded, you were too terrified to answer, at first. You just shook your head and couldn't even look at me. Then finally you lifted your eyes and weakly said, "He killed me." Do you remember that?

"Aha. I am so sorry I scared you, Mommy. I could not help it."

I know, my love, I know.

I cannot recall where I read that the premonition about one's pending death is not uncommon for adults as well as for children. The Chassidut says that the soul knows about its departure from this life 40 days before its actual departure. Is it true, Gili? Some of your writings and conversations indicate that it might be, especially the statement you made on Thursday, a day before you were killed.

"We were in the kitchen. You were selecting Chanukah candles in my favorite colors, pink and blue, to light up, when I said to you: 'Mommy, I know that you and Normi don't believe in God, but I thought about it, and I decided that I do believe in God. I hope it's OK with you."

And I, deeply moved by your mature demeanor, said: "I respect your beliefs. If you believe that there is a God, then there is a God for you." You flashed to me one of your glorious smiles, as if you sighed in relief. Did you anticipate an argument?

"No, not really. I was just so happy that my new belief was accepted."

SPIRITUAL QUEST

I wonder, where do premonitions come from? What are they? Is my need to understand the nature of premonitions an attempt (perhaps a futile one) to understand what happened? to know the answer to the "Why" question? Perhaps by accepting either that we have the mental ability to foresee the future or that our "psyche" senses a predetermined future, my sense of guilt and self-blame would be diminished. In other words, if your death was predetermined by Divine intervention, then I could not have protected you. Were you meant to have only a short visit on this earth? Is my spiritual search merely a pathetic solution to my overwhelming feelings of guilt, shame, and self-blame? Or was your death, my most life-shattering experience, an awakening to Life on its most grandiose scale?

My old self died with your body, my love. But from the ashes of my old self, a new self emerged to the calling of your spirit. Not all traumatic experiences are transformational—I know that firsthand. But your death definitely transformed me and my life forever. In my previous life (the life I had before you were killed), I would have attempted to provide a "psychological-philosophical" explanation. Today, I cannot revert to this way of thinking. Any attempt to explain any event by excluding a Divine intervention or intention sounds to me arrogant, and there is no room for it in my new conceptualization of life and death. I want to believe that the universe has purpose and reason: that we live in an organized universe, where, as the Chassidut says, every leaf that falls off a tree falls at a particular moment, at a particular spot, at the only time and at the only moment it was supposed to fall. Every event reflects Divine intervention and is individually supervised. There are no accidents in this world.

I'll give an example of a perception that I could have accepted in my "previous professional life" prior to your death but that I cannot fully accept anymore: In describing the dynamics of the continuing bond with the deceased child, Klass (1988, 1993) examines the nature of solace. Bereaved parents, he writes, find long-term solace in continuing interaction with the inner representation of their dead child. Klass goes on to describe the following phenomena as involving a sense of the presence of the deceased: experiencing hallucinations in any of the senses, believing in the deceased person's continuing active influence on thoughts and events, or consciously incorporating characteristics or virtues of the dead into the self.

I can relate to these descriptions of experiences, although not to all components of the inner representation. I conceptualize my experiences differently (see Chapter 8). I do not agree that we hallucinate a "visitation." My belief is similar to that of Sandra Bertman (1991), who said that death ends a life but not a relationship and that the grief work (or part of it, as I think) is to relocate the deceased in inner space and time.

I do believe that your soul as well as mine has an independent and eternal existence. Our soul, our life energy, survives bodily death. And, as such, it may continue to interact with and influence the living in the physical world. Therefore I do not believe that I hallucinated when I heard your voice whispering in my ear; or when I felt Norm's tapping me lightly on my head, while he was taking his last breaths, and telling me, "I'm fine, my darling, I'm fine"; or during many other experiences that I have had, thanks to your interactions with me since you died. I firmly believe that the bond between parent and child is not severed at the time of death but is strengthened. Death separated only our bodies, not our souls. I am convinced that your soul, my love, survived the death of your body. I believe, therefore, that you did not lose your ability and desire to communicate with me or with others. You were always a powerful communicator—and you still are. But now, it's up to me to sharpen my listening and other perceptual abilities.

My new perception has been reinforced by *Hello From Heaven* (Guggenheim & Guggenheim, 1996), which examines thousands of testimonials of bereaved people and their experiences of communications from their deceased loved ones. The Guggenheims call this phenomenon After Death Communication (ADC). What do you think, my love? Am I a lunatic for finding types of thinking that do not acknowledge Divine intervention to be too arrogant, and not at all satisfactory or meaningful in explaining what I have been experiencing since you passed away from this physical world?

"Mommy, I can tell you only this: Trust your gut feeling. Trust what feels truthful and real to you. You don't need to convince me about your integrity or that your experiences were real. Once you have an experience, you are forever and at once separated from those who have only read or heard about it. No matter how much you doubt whether what happened to you was real, imagined, or whether it was the result of your wishful thinking, deep in your heart, you know the answer. But it's up to you."

PART II

End and Beginning: Life Without Gili

CHAPTER 5

My Search for Answers

"I told you to trust your gut feeling. So, tell me, Ima: How do you feel? Talk to me. Ani makshiva (I'm listening)."

I will tell you, my love. There is so much of what I have learned that I want to share with you. *But the most important thing I want to tell you is that nothing in my professional or personal experience had prepared me for the devastation of your death.* So in an attempt to make some sense of what happened, I turned inward, to observe myself; and outward, first to the literature, and then to discussions with different people, including mental health professionals, rabbis, bereaved parents, and others who had suffered loss. Let me unfold what I found in my search.

"Are these readings and discussions part of your introduction to your concept of parental bereavement?"

Exactly. I'll show you and the reader how this search led me to develop my own understanding of the process of parental bereavement.

"I see that you are going to put your lecturer's hat on. That's OK, Mommy, I know when to 'sign-off.' But I'll eavesdrop from time to time."

I'd like that, Metuka sheli. From time to time, I'll talk to you directly, and at other times I'll talk about you, if it's OK with you.

"It's fine, Mommy. Go on."

*   *   *

Before I begin, let me clarify the use of certain terms. Some authors provide separate definitions for the terms *grief* and *mourning*, treating them as complementary processes of bereavement. Wolfelt (1994), for instance, defines *mourning* as the external expression of grief, or "grief gone public," and *grief* as the internal meaning given to the external event, death (1994, pp. 26–27).

I will use the terms *grief* and *mourning* interchangeably, because I believe that these processes exist on a continuum rather than being distinctly different from one another. Grief reactions are more introverted reactions, similar to the inward steps in my model of parental bereavement (see Chapter 8). Mourning is characterized by more extroverted reactions, similar to the outward steps in my model. Bereavement refers to the general state of one who has suffered loss and includes both grief and mourning, both Inward and Outward Steps.

TRADITIONAL THEORIES OF BEREAVEMENT: THE MEDICAL MODEL

Freud's *Mourning and Melancholia* (1917/1957) is one of the best examples of the medical type of thinking and probably the most influential work on mourning. Freud gave a generic description of mourning; he did not develop a specific model of the process of mourning. Instead, he described bereavement as a general process that first causes disintegration of mental and behavioral processes, then leads to integration of the self into social life once again. Freud claimed that the behaviors typical of bereaved people would be described as "pathological" in circumstances other than bereavement but should be considered "normal" as part of the grieving process. (In my view, because our society values "stoic" behavior, any behavior that expresses emotions intensely and continues for what is judged to be "a long time" is considered to be "pathological.")

Freud described "grief work," as he termed the grieving process, as occurring in simultaneous phases. The grief work consists, according to Freud, of confrontation between the illusion that the deceased is still alive (the denial of the death) and the acknowledgment of the new reality. I agree with his perception of grief as a simultaneous process rather than a chronological, or linear, one.

Let me clarify the difference between simultaneous and linear, or chronological, phases or stages with my own experience: I never felt only one type of emotion at a time. If I interpret *phase* or *stage* as an emotional state with one distinct, overpowering emotion, then I never felt, for example, despair all the time; or after despair, anger. This would be a linear, chronological, process, as some writers (e.g., Kübler-Ross) have described. Instead, I felt and still feel many types of emotions at the same time. I felt despair, anger, protest, deep sadness, and many more emotions and thoughts all at once, simultaneously. Silverman (Klass, Silverman, & Nickman, 1996), in her discussion about the continuing bond with the deceased child, stressed the notion of simultaneity. She asserted that it is possible to be bereft and not bereft simultaneously—the same way that it is possible to feel the child present in and absent from one's life at the same time.

Bowlby (1980) took Freud's description of the process of mourning a bit further and developed a model of mourning—again, a generic, nonspecific description of the process of bereavement. Bowlby described three stages in the process of grieving: (1) protest, where the bereaved person protests against what happened to him or her; (2) despair, which follows protest; and (3) detachment, where the survivor detaches him- or herself from the deceased in order to recover from the grief.

I certainly experienced the emotions that are described in Bowlby's work. But again, I do not agree with his attempt to superficially separate what is experienced simultaneously into distinct stages, nor with the idea that the bereaved have to detach themselves from those they mourn in order to be able to attach themselves to a new person, or "object."

By contrast, Klass (1993; Klass et al., 1996) contended that continuing the relationship with the deceased child is normal and healthy, and that severing the relationship is unhealthy. Continuing the relationship or the bond with the deceased child can be described through its psychological components, such as thinking of the child, dreaming about her, and feeling her presence, or through more concrete, physical components, such as mentioning her name, decorating the house or office with her pictures, and commemorating her in various other ways. I agree that the continuing relationship is an extremely important factor for the parent's well-being. Of course, as with any set of behaviors, we may attempt to define what should be considered "healthy" and what should not. In principle, any behavior that causes or promotes extreme isolation of the bereaved parent or that excludes or causes harm to others in the family cannot be considered healthy. It is hard to define in exact terms what "extreme" isolation or harm means in this case, because the definition is subjective. We need to ask ourselves from which perspective the condition is defined: from the bereaved parent's or from the observer's? Also, when can isolation be considered extreme? Is there a timetable? My answer is: The bereaved parent knows when her behavior has become extreme. She knows when her withdrawal has become self-defeating and even self-destructive. Also, those who knew the bereaved parent well before the death of the child also know, by comparison, whether this behavior has reached extreme levels. Although the extreme behavior may appear to be sudden, it is a gradual process. In terms of my model of inward and outward steps (Chapter 8), extreme isolation, or "unhealthy" behavior, can be described as a result of imbalance between inward and outward steps—when more or mainly inward steps have been taken by the parent, with no or few outward steps. However, one should not confuse extreme withdrawal or isolation that is unhealthy with withdrawal that may *appear* to the observer to be "unhealthy" or extreme but for the parent is a necessity for survival. It is the parent's perspective that should take precedence.

As I said earlier, we each mourn in a different way. What is obviously a necessity for my survival is not necessarily a necessity for another parent's

94 End and Beginning: Life Without Gili

survival. There are many factors that play a part in determining whether a parent will readjust to life. There are no timetables to tell us how long we should grieve, no sets of rules to tell us how to behave!

I know that there are traditions in different cultures (see Irish, Lundquist, & Nelsen, 1993) that dictate both a timetable and certain customs for mourning. For instance, Jews mourn for seven days, thirty days, and a year, with specific customs assigned to each period of time. But these traditions were designed for children who mourn their parents, not the other way around. I resented the fact that there were no special prayers to say for my child, only for my father. Therefore, I felt a need to compose my own prayer for her.

Just as I had to find my own way of mourning Gili, so, too, I had to find my own theory of mourning.

The Concept of Recovery

Many researchers (e.g., Figley, 1989; Furman, 1984; Gilliland & James, 1993; Hundley, 1993; Kübler-Ross, 1969; Lahad & Ayalon, 1995; Rando, 1986a, 1986b; Schaefer & Lyons, 1988; Schneider, 1984; Worden, 1991; Worden & Monahan, 1993) have a view similar to Freud's about bereavement. Within this medical model of thinking, the process of mourning is treated as a necessary means of reaching the goal of "recovery": It is assumed that movement through the process of mourning can be completed and that there is an implied timetable for successful recovery. I do not agree with these assumptions. To begin with, I do not think that mourning is either an unusual reaction or a sign that something is wrong. On the contrary, mourning is an expected, normal, and healthy reaction. I also think that the concept of mourning should not be generalized, as it is in these medical models: The reaction of mourning is specific and unique in its characteristics to the particular type of loss. Mourning for a child is a different process from grieving for other loved ones. I think that parents grieve for their children as long as they live (see also Edelstein, 1984; Klass, 1988; Klass et al., 1996; Raphael, 1983).

My reactions to Norm's death were very different from my reactions to Gili's death. I watched Norm dying of lung cancer. Although one is never truly prepared for the final departure from this physical world, nevertheless he and I had some time to adjust to the unavoidable end. We had time (although it is never enough) to make preparations, to bond in devotion, and to love to the fullest. In the process of taking care of Norm, I discovered a new life force emerging in me; and when Norm passed over that life force continued surging, growing, and evolving. Contrary to what I felt when

Gili was killed, my self didn't die with Norm; there was already a new self in emergence. And despite my acute pain, I was not devastated. I was only painfully aware of the differences—then and now. I had closed a complete circle of a relationship with Norm, but I did not have a chance to do so with my daughter.

The death of a child is the death of the parent's future, both illusions and possibilities. This is especially true when the bond between the parent and the child was particularly strong and when the child was of the same sex as the parent. For myself and other parents in this situation, there may be a strong tendency to perceive the child as an "ideal" extension of one's self. This is not the case with the death of a spouse or a parent. With the loss of Gili, I lost my future, too; and with the loss of my future, I lost my hope. And hope is embedded in the future, not in the past. One cannot live without a future nor without hope.

As parents' lives shift toward different directions, such as other relationships or other occupations, their external expressions of grief may become less prominent in their daily behavior. But wherever there has been a loving relationship, the internal grief continues, although at times with less intensity than during the first years.

Solace might be found in changes that take place in the parent's life, including changes in beliefs. But the grief reaction never completely disappears. I don't know if any grief reaction ever disappears, regardless of the type of loss, but the grief for a dead child is especially severe.

Stages, Phases, and Tasks

Many medical models of bereavement imply that the process of bereavement is accomplished in a series of stages (Kübler-Ross, 1969), phases (Sanders, 1992; Schneider, 1984), or tasks (Corr, Nabe, & Corr, 1997; Worden, 1991). Kübler-Ross (1969) developed a five-stage model based on her observations of terminally ill patients, concluding that a dying person goes through these stages in the following order: (1) denial and isolation, (2) anger, (3) bargaining, (4) depression, and (5) acceptance. Kübler-Ross suggested that these stages, mainly linear, can also be applied to those who have lost a loved one. Although "stage" models, such as the one proposed by Kübler-Ross, have been criticized for their limited and rigid scope and for their tendency to conceptualize grief as a passive process (see Attig, 1996; Rando, 1993; Worden, 1991), they are still the best-known theories and as such require some attention.

Similar to the stage models are the phase models, also influenced by the medical way of thinking. Schneider (1984, 1994) argued that his phase model, which is not specific for bereaved parents, implies that grief has a transient quality that may endure for a few moments or for a much longer period of time. He described the grief process in terms of concentric circles, rather than linear movement, through six phases: (1) coping, (2) awareness of the loss, (3) perspective, (4) integration, (5) reformulating, and (6) transformation. Each phase can be repeated as the bereaved progresses toward resolution of the grief. Schneider claimed that due to its linear nature, the stage approach lacks that movement. But still, there is no description of simultaneous "phases" or simultaneous emotions.

Bowlby (1980), one of the pioneers in writing about loss, developed a phase model of mourning that is based on his earlier theory of attachment. The phases are believed to occur as an "overall sequence," although there may be oscillation between them at various points. The phases are: (1) numbing; (2) yearning and searching, which is characterized by intense longing, deep distress, and anger; (3) disorganization, which entails a conscious examination of "how" and "why"; and (4) reorganization, or a "redefinition" of both self and situation, which is both cognitive and affective in nature. Bowlby's phases are similar to categories of feelings, thoughts, behaviors, or actions.

Rando (1993), preferring to discuss the mourning process in terms of reactions, delineated three psychological reactions to grief: (1) avoidance, (2) confrontation, and (3) re-establishment. Rando indicated that re-establishment is a gradual process that overlaps with the phase of confrontation, often producing guilt and anxiety as the bereaved attempts to move forward. I can relate to Rando's concept of "reactions," but she, too, assumes that the grieving process of parents, although it has no timetable, is eventually resolved. In other words, there is "recovery" from mourning; and in Rando's model re-establishment, or resolution of the grieving process, is accomplished by relinquishing the old attachments to the old assumptive world, which includes the detachment from assumptions one held about the deceased. I wonder to what extent does detachment from assumptions about the deceased not imply detachment from the deceased himself or herself.

Another variation on the stages-of-grief framework, not specific to bereaved parents, can be found in Worden's work. Rejecting the stage or phase models as passive, Worden (1991) developed his four-task model of mourning, which he perceived as more active and amenable to therapeutic intervention. The four tasks are: (1) to accept the reality of the loss, both intellectually and emotionally; (2) to work through the pain of grief; (3) to adjust to an environment in which the deceased is missing; and (4) to emotionally relocate the deceased and move on with life. According to Worden, mourning is complete when these four tasks are accomplished. And although he cautioned against the use of timetables, he nevertheless said that the mourning process lasts a minimum of 1 year and often much longer. He acknowledged that there is always cognizance of the loss and therefore, in one sense, mourning is never complete, especially the mourning of parents who have lost a child. It is a long-term process and one can never return to a "pre-grief state."

I find many points of correspondence with my own experience in many of these theorists' writings, but I do not agree with some of their fundamental assumptions about the grief process. It is my conviction that parental bereavement is a never-ending process, with no detachment from the deceased child and no timetables, distinct stages, phases, or tasks to be accomplished. Although the parent's grief reactions may appear extreme for extended periods of time, they should nevertheless be considered normal to this unique type of loss. Definitions of what constitutes "healthy grieving" and "recovery" are inappropriate, and references to "pathological" and "complicated" grief reactions should be used rarely and with great caution.

In summary, although each model of bereavement defines the process differently, they all follow a similar pattern. They all attempt to explain the mourning process as though it were an illness with a beginning, a middle, and an end—with stages, phases, or tasks to be achieved in the progression toward recovery. I, instead, explain parental mourning as a process of readjustment to life with loss, which lasts a lifetime. This process progresses through simultaneous inward and outward steps. Most of the time many emotions and thoughts are experienced at once.

I knew right away that Gili was dead. I did not experience any distinct stage of grief at any given moment. (Nor did I observe, when Norm was dying, that he went through any such stages.) I did not feel any "denial," "bargaining," or "acceptance." I do sometimes pretend (not deny), especially when I see children getting off a schoolbus, that she, too, will get off this bus and will run to me with open arms as she always used to do. With my imagination I pretend, and for a brief moment only, because it hurts too much to hold the image longer. I never "accepted" her death. I have not observed any "acceptance" in other parents either.

We never really "accept" the fact that our beloved children have died. We acknowledge the death of our children and our new reality. In the best case there is a readjustment, or an adaptation. This is not a semantic difference. It is a difference in dynamics. "Acceptance" implies acquiescence and passivity. "Readjustment" connotes integration and growth, activity and change.

THE NONPROFESSIONAL LITERATURE

The previous section explored the contributions of mental health professionals to an understanding of bereavement. But writers in other fields, and bereaved parents, also have something important to contribute. The description of my inner search would not be complete without describing some of the other readings that have changed forever the way I view my life after Gili's death. If my readings of the professional literature served to inform, confirm, or contradict my experience and knowledge about mourning, then my readings of the nonprofessional literature served to challenge my worldview and my entire belief system.

Before Gili was killed, my belief system could have been summarized in a few sentences: There must be "something bigger than man" in the universe; and that "something bigger" might be God. But I was not sure that there is a God and especially that our lives are governed by some indescribable entity. However, I kept an open mind to the possibility that someday, somehow, I would be convinced of the existence of God. I believed that although the universe appears to have purpose and some order, to some extent chaos and arbitrariness do exist. I believed that it is within our power to change the course of our lives. (What an arrogant perception!) I thought that death is the end of life. I did not believe in the survival of the soul, although I was familiar with spiritual, religious, and anecdotal writings about reincarnation, rebirth, near-death experiences, after-death experiences, and mediums' and channelors' communications with the spirit world. I read these works sometimes in fascination, sometimes in boredom, but always with skepticism. I never felt a need to "communicate" with any of my deceased relatives, including my father (did I need to hear him yelling at me again?), or with friends. And even my fatalism was not well grounded in any theory.

So when on Thursday night, just a day before Gili was killed, she came into the kitchen where Norm and I sat and told me, "Ima, I know that you and Norm don't believe in God, but I thought about it, and I hope it's OK with you, because I decided that I believe in God," I felt unprepared. She then added: "Do you think that God exists?"

And my answer was: God exists for those who believe in His existence. Norm cringed when I said that. He did not believe that there is a God at all. What could I have told my child then? I was ashamed that I did not have a better, more reassuring answer for her. How I wish that we could have had the opportunity to have this conversation today . . . face-to-face.

Religious and Spiritual Writings

The first spiritual book I read was given to me by one of Norm's friends—
When Bad Things Happen to Good People, by Rabbi Harold Kushner (1981).
Kushner's concept of arbitrariness in this world—the idea that this universe,
which was created by God, can be chaotic and that therefore accidents do
happen—was not what I wanted to hear. I felt more comforted by the
Kabbalistic–Chassidic notion that "everything has its right time" and that
there is a reason and purpose to everything. The Chassidic rabbi with whom
I started studying once told me that every leaf that falls off the tree falls off
exactly at the moment when and the place where it was supposed to fall.
This philosophy seemed to attribute more meaning not only to Gili's death
but also to her life. My readings in the *Tanya*, the main composition of
Lubavitch Chassidism, became one of the main sources of comfort for me.
The *Tanya*, which was composed by Rabbi Schneur Zalman of Liadi in 1797,
founder of Chabad–Lubavitch Chassidism, is the most authoritative text
of Chabad Chassidism. The book includes interpretations of the Bible as
well as concepts that are relevant to the modern Jew searching for his or
her "philosophical orientation."

An additional important source of comfort was the realization that
psychology has begun to recognize and explore issues of spirituality (Attig,
1996; Becvar, 1997; Bertman, 1991). This may have occurred in response to
New Age philosophies, but in any case, it marks a return to psychology's
roots in philosophy.

While there is an emerging literature about spirituality in psychology,
important contributions have been made by laypersons. (Some of this literature is questionable, however, and should be read with caution.) I started
devouring books that attempted to provide proof that death is only a transition to another life, that the soul survives death, and that we can communicate with the deceased. The first book to affect my life forever was *We Don't
Die* (Martin & Romanowski, 1988), which described George Anderson's conversations with the Other Side. Anderson is a psychic medium who "chan-
nels" messages from the "Other Side." He works mostly with bereaved parents. I later went to Long Island to meet George Anderson. I came back a
person with a changed view. I could feel Gili's presence in his room, which
was filled mainly with bereaved parents. Another book that sent me searching to contact another medium (I was still not completely convinced that Gili's
soul had survived her body) was *To Dance with Angels* (Pendelton & Pendel-
tons, 1990). I had numerous telephone sessions with Thomas Jacobson, who
channeled a spirit called Dr. Peebles; I even went to California to meet with
Jacobson. These were some of my most profound experiences.

Norm was concerned that I was becoming confused, that some charla-
tans were taking advantage of my vulnerability. Was I confused? Not at
all. In fact, these contacts helped to sharpen my perception and focus my
attention. They forced me to move, physically as well as mentally; to re-
connect with the outside world. They challenged my previous beliefs and
consolidated a new, firmer belief in God and His acts.

Bereaved Parents' Writings

It seemed to me, at different times during my continuous search, that I was
open to different types of writings. In general, I found little comfort in books
written by bereaved parents; something was missing. If the parent's
struggle to survive came through, then their child's personality did not; or
I could not find any principles that I could apply to myself.

However, here and there I found a few ideas or descriptions in those
writings that "spoke" to me. One such book that affected me deeply 6 years
after Gili's death, and would not have affected me the same way earlier,
was *There Is Also Hope in Bereavement* (Givoli, 1993). What affected me so
deeply was the passion and vulnerability with which this father talked
about his suffering. Although he and I shared some similar emotions, we
arrived at different conclusions about life and death. That was fascinat-
ing, too.

But I already knew that I had to write my own book. I knew that my
book would not be complete without mentioning my increased awareness
of unusual occurrences in my waking hours and during sleep. Starting
when I was 6 years old, I developed the habit of recording my dreams, and
this allowed me to be acutely aware of the change in my consciousness
levels. I still had "normal" dreams, when I could fall asleep, but I also
started having what I called "visitations" from Gili (and later from Norm)
when not asleep but not fully awake either. I could hear noises from outside, I was aware of my body lying in bed; but I could also feel her as if she
were alive. I could touch her, smell and hear her! And at the same time I
knew that I was experiencing something very unusual because Gili was
dead. I started paying attention to messages from her. It has affected the
way I interpret my dreams and the dreams of other bereaved people.

I received many messages from Gili. Some were as dramatic as a "kiss"
sound left on my tape recorder. One was a short story that Gili dictated to
me in a dream-like state. Another was a rare book on past lives to which
she directed me during one very detailed dream-like state, so I would be
finally convinced that she was communicating with me. In that particular
incidence, I was shown the book cover and the last name of the author:
Finkelstein (1985). This is what enabled me to find that book. However, in

spite of this disclosure, I am not ready to recount all of these special experiences. I treasure them too much to share them with everybody. Perhaps when I meet bereaved parents who can relate to my experiences, I will share them.

My goal in telling our story is to help bereaved parents and those who work with the bereaved to better understand parental bereavement, and it is sufficient to know that such unusual occurrences are usual for bereaved parents. Some may be afraid to admit such experiences to others for fear of being ridiculed or misunderstood. Others may ignore the messages that are placed in front of them to serve, perhaps, as guiding lights.

*   *   *

I am talking to Gili in silence, and in my mind's ear I hear her response. But I am also aware of the date. Very soon, we would have celebrated another birthday. I cannot even envision her as a young woman. For me, Gili will forever remain an 11-year-old girl. Very bright and mature far beyond her age, but nevertheless, 11. Only I get older; she will remain forever a child. So, do I talk to her as a 19-year-old going on 20? Or do I continue talking to her as an 11-year-old going on 40? I can hear Gili's response. She would have said: "Just talk to me, Mommy. Please don't cry; our hearts are ageless." And Gili would be right. Our hearts, our souls, are ageless.

CHAPTER 6

Delving Deeper: Reactions to Loss

One way of coping with grief—one congenial to my temperament and profession—is to read about bereavement and to search for intellectual answers. To make sense of Gili's death and my feelings, I delved deeper into the relevant literature in psychology. This chapter summarizes my continuing journey through the professional literature, made in an attempt to help myself and others by gaining a better understanding of the process of parental grief.

EMOTIONAL REACTIONS TO LOSS: WITHDRAWAL, EXTERNALIZATION, AND AVOIDANCE

Much has been written about bereavement from the perspective of psychology as well as related fields. A valuable perspective may be found in the work of Larson (1993), who discussed the job-related stress reactions and coping responses of those who work with bereaved people in *The Helper's Journey*. Larson pointed out how for those working with clients facing loss of various kinds, stress evolves and is maintained through the simultaneous interaction of interpersonal and intrapersonal characteristics.

In a similar way, sources of stress for bereaved people can be interpersonal—for instance, expectations to behave in certain ways "appropriate" for bereaved people—or intrapersonal—for example, when the grieving person blames him- or herself for the death or internalizes the expectations of others about "appropriate" mourning. The inner conflict between one's own identified needs and the internalized societal expectations may result in tremendous stress. A closely related set of ideas is expressed in Rubin's (1993) two-track model of parental bereavement: Here the relationship (interpersonal) dimension refers to the parent's very valued and charged relationship with the deceased child, and the function (intrapersonal) dimension refers to the disorganization and reorganization of psychological, biological, and social functioning of the bereaved parents.

Larson (1993; Larson & Chastain, 1990) identified three typical patterns of reaction to loss that are manifested throughout one's entire life, as coping styles, not just immediately following the loss. One general pattern is withdrawal and retreat inside the self, which is often termed a "depressed" reaction. A second reaction is more "manic" in nature: One turns outward and externalizes the grief in an almost feverish manner. A third typical reaction is "avoidance" of talking about the deceased and the loss, pretending to the external world that nothing has happened. In my experience, this reaction can be found both in bereaved parents (usually temporary) and in those who know them.

Avoidance

Some parents and grandparents who lose a child cannot face the pain, and they run away. Some don't even mention their child's name. Like my mother, my mother who suffered multiple losses: five children (two before I was born); her own mother, who died delivering her into this world; her father, who died two years later; a large family, the only relatives she had left, who died in the Nazi concentration camps; her first husband (my father); Gili, her beloved only granddaughter; and her second husband. My mother's motto is: You should never look back, only forward.

It hurts, because I do look back, and I want her to say Gili's name. I want her to talk about her. And I want to be able to talk about Gili with her. It took me a while to accept that we react in very different ways to loss. How anyone reacts depends on upbringing, previous life experiences, beliefs, tradition, and culture. And, of course, on the depth of love—and sometimes of conflict—that we feel for or had with that child. Some, like my mom, have built a wall, so to speak, in order to shut out that unbearable pain so they won't have to feel it. Not looking back is their only way to survive, I guess—the most effective barrier to the feelings of loss that threatens to overwhelm them.

I remember one bereaved mother who came to see me shortly after her teenage son committed suicide. Her temporary style of coping with her grief was by running away from her surviving family to a place and job where nobody knew her or her son. She told me that she put a picture of her deceased son on her desk, and when asked by co-workers if this was her son, she would make up stories about him as though he were still alive. This mother was perfectly aware of what she was doing; she just needed "a break," as she told me—a break from deep sadness and from the pity of others. This was her way of putting her grief "on an upper shelf," as I call it, to be dealt with later.

The avoidance patterns of those surrounding the bereaved parent, however, are less likely to be temporary. Most of the people around me—colleagues, some friends, and family—still act as though Gili and Norm never existed, or as if I am a single woman with no past instead of a bereaved mother and grieving widow. It is hard to know whether this is avoidance or an extreme interpretation of privacy; it might be both. For some people, such as the client mentioned above, it might be avoidance—at least temporary avoidance of dealing with intense emotions. But for others, bereaved as well as nonbereaved, this behavior may signify more of a cultural/philosophical stance; they may believe that loss is a private matter, not to be discussed in public. Any attempt to talk about the deceased or even to mention their death may be interpreted as an invasion of privacy. Clearly, behaviors and attitudes are affected by values and beliefs.

The other interpretation, of course, is that people who pretend that nothing has happened actually live in denial of death. But I doubt that there is true denial of death. Although denial is a powerful defense mechanism against internal conflict, for it to persist in the face of death, the mourner needs to be completely unaware of his or her internal state of mind. Life and death are on the same continuum: To truly deny the existence of one end, it is necessary to deny the existence of the other, a feat that is beyond us as living beings. Paradoxically, our reluctance to cultivate an awareness of death limits our ability to appreciate life. As Betty Friedan (1993) has said so bluntly, "Focusing on death is a way of becoming fully alive" (p. 543).

*   *   *

I could never run away from the pain, although I wanted to do so many times. Instead, I looked straight into the eye of horror; this tends to be my way of coping with what frightens me most. I talk about Gili even with those who do not want to hear. I find all kinds of reasons to mention her name every day. This behavior is not dictated by compulsion. I made a conscious decision to continue talking about Gili. It is my way of commemorating her, but it is also a message that I'm trying to deliver: Gili was, still is, and will always be extremely important to me. Her life had a meaning that her untimely death did not diminish. Parents usually talk about their children. Why should I, who used to brag about both of my children, be prevented now from talking about one of them only because she is not with us in physical form? It's not easy to talk about Gili in the past tense. But what do I know about her present? What kind of a future can I describe? It's not getting easier.

Pre-Traumatic Factors in Coping with Loss

How individuals respond to trauma depends in part on their level of functioning before the traumatic experience. Studies on the effects of various pre-existing factors on individuals' responses to trauma have found that factors such as pre-trauma maladjustment, a troubled family history, and general feelings of helplessness increased the likelihood of developing a post-traumatic stress disorder (see Bootzin & Acocella, 1984). In short, a person who had difficulties adjusting to life without trauma will be more likely to have difficulties in adjusting to life after a traumatic event. Not surprisingly, coping styles and attributional styles also affect the response to trauma. For instance, using an analytical style, which focuses on the problem, as opposed to an emotional style, which applies wishful thinking, denial, or emotional venting in problem solving, protects more effectively against the development of post-traumatic stress.

Studies on bereavement (e.g., Figley, 1985, 1989; Schneider, 1984; Wass, 1984) suggest that individuals and families who were emotionally healthy before the loss of the loved one cope better than those who were emotionally dysfunctional before their loss. Schneider (1984) listed nine factors that influence the mourning process: (1) the age of the survivor at the time of the loss, (2) the type of loss and type of attachment, (3) the number of losses (people tend to shut down if they experience too many losses in a short period of time), (4) the degree of support in existing relationships, (5) the pre-loss personality structure, (6) the nature of the death (sudden death is thought of as harder to grieve for than anticipated death), (7) the amount of control the survivor had over the loss (e.g., losing a loved one to an accident versus initiating a divorce), (8) the time at which the helping professional is contacted, and (9) the existing framework of the helping professional.

The number and variety of these factors help to explain why everyone who experiences a similar traumatic event does not respond in the same way. In my work with bereaved clients I have found that although some shared feelings and symptoms may be found among people who have suffered similar losses, no two losses are the same. Many factors affect the reactions to loss, and I would add to Schneider's list the belief system of the bereaved as well as the sex of the survivor and the deceased. A child usually identifies with the same-sex parent, and this is a reciprocal relationship: The same-sex parent also lives (and re-lives) in many ways through the child. For this and other reasons, the sex of both the child and parent are important factors in determining the course of mourning. For instance, because of the identification of the parent with the same-sex child, there might be a deeper sense of loss of the future: A mother may expect to re-live her wedding day through her daughter's anticipated wedding. Or of the past: A father may experience a profound feeling of loss of his own youth, of his past, when his son has died. Yet another factor, regardless of sex, is whether the child was considered "the father's" or "the mother's" child.

Sudden Death and Traumatic Grief

While each individual response to trauma is unique, there are also similarities according to the type of trauma suffered. Studies of Vietnam veterans and survivors of civil and terrorist violence in Northern Ireland indicate that "re-experiencing symptoms," such as intrusive memories, nightmares, and startle reactions, are most common in those who have witnessed or suffered acts of abusive violence (Bootzin & Acocella, 1984). This, in my personal as well as professional experience, is similar to the reactions of parents whose child was murdered or killed in a car crash. Even when the parents are not direct victims of the crime or accident, they may nevertheless have similar reactions to those who suffer directly from a violent, traumatic event because of their close relationship and identification with their children.

*   *   *

I was not in the car with Gili when the crash occurred, but I was sitting at home only 30 feet away from where it happened, and so I heard the screeching of the tires and the crunch of metal crashing into metal. I feel as if these sounds will continue echoing in my ears for the rest of my life. The visual images, the thoughts and emotions of those moments, are imprinted on my eyes and on every cell of my being. And had I not been physically present to hear and see them, my imagination would have supplied them. As the indirect victim, I exhibited all the symptoms typical of a traumatized person: heightened anxiety, nightmares, startle reactions, and so on. It is not surprising that recent studies have sought to combine the concept of bereavement with the concept of post-traumatic stress (Lord & Mercer, 1997; Rando & Figley, 1996).

*   *   *

That the nature of death is a critical factor in the mourning process is reflected in the three categories of grief identified by G. Sprang and McNeil (1995): (1) grief as a result of death by natural causes, (2) traumatic grief, and (3) stigmatized grief. Responses to AIDS-related death and suicide are conceptualized as stigmatized grief. Responses to murder, traffic fatalities, and community disasters are considered traumatic grief.

It is important to acknowledge the nature of the death in order to understand the differences in the mourning process. For every parent, the loss of a child is the worst thing that can happen, but the intensity of grief can be compounded by the shock and surprise of sudden, unanticipated death (Rando, 1986a, 1986b, 1994; Worden & Monahan, 1993). This is especially true in the death of a child. Parkes (1985), noting the unique response of bereaved persons following the unanticipated death of a loved one, identified an "unexpected grief syndrome"—that is, sudden and untimely death is characterized by delayed emotional reaction and moderate to high anxiety. Although his description of this "syndrome" is, in the tradition of the psychoanalytic study of grief, focused on "pathological" variants and psychiatric maladjustment to loss, it is nonetheless an acknowledgment that the grief response may vary significantly as a function of the circumstances surrounding the death.

In a discussion specifically of parental bereavement, Worden (1991) listed eight typical reactions in cases of sudden death: (1) numbness, or a sense of unreality, which may last a long time; (2) an exacerbated sense of guilt; (3) an extremely strong need to blame; (4) delayed grief and victimization due to involvement with legal or medical authorities; (5) a sense of helplessness; (6) heightened agitation and adrenaline secretion; (7) a sense of unfinished business; and (8) an overwhelming need to understand what happened.

On Guilt, Blame, and Shame. *Guilt* is an especially prominent reaction among parents whose young children have died. It was Norm's observation that guilt has its own impetus to keep it going. Surviving our children is a reversal of the natural order—we are not supposed to outlive our children. We, as caregivers, are expected to protect and, when needed, save our children's lives. When we fail to protect or save, we are often overcome by a profound sense of guilt that we may carry with us for the rest of our lives. This sense of guilt is triggered by the parents' perceptions of themselves as caregivers and is sustained by their values. Usually, such feelings of guilt have very little to do with the actual events that caused the child's death.

Guilt is often accompanied by *blame*. The issue of blame is particularly salient in cases of sudden, unexpected, and human-induced loss. Weinberg (1994), for instance, found that self-blame, other-blame, and the combination of the two (dual-blame) were more common responses in persons whose loved ones died as a result of sudden or "unnatural" causes as compared to persons whose loved ones died of "natural" causes. Certainly I have felt both guilt and dual-blame. And at times I still do.

In myself and in other bereaved parents, I have observed that *shame*, which often springs from guilt but is a more painful sense of guilt and of unworthiness, is one of the most overwhelming emotions in parental grief. Finkbeiner (1996), a bereaved mother herself who interviewed other bereaved parents, claimed that *guilt* was the most overwhelming emotion even years after the death of her child. I think that with regard to the loss of a child, *shame* is a fundamental fear of condemnation by others for failing to protect your loved ones—for failing to fulfill your social role as parent. Shame causes a decrease in self-esteem. I have observed in my work with bereaved parents that low self-esteem and lack of feelings of self-worth are typical—not atypical, as Worden (1991) claims. For a long time after Gili died, I used to shy away from making eye contact; shame, I feel, interfered with my social re-engagement. For all these reasons, shame deserves special attention.

*   *   *

For years, I felt ashamed for failing in my duty to protect Gili's life. The shame cut me off from others and deepened my sense of guilt for surviving her death. Regarding Norm's death, I don't feel any shame or guilt. Is it because there is less of a sense of control over an illness than there is in a killing? Is it because of the different perception of my role as mother as compared to my role as spouse? As a mother, I am expected to protect and save my child, not to outlive her; this is not so as a spouse.

On Organ and/or Tissue Donation. A special aspect of parental bereavement is the compounded grief felt by parents who have donated their children's organs or tissues. The profound bond between parent and child continues beyond the grave, and one characteristic of this continuing relationship is the bond that these parents often develop with the recipient(s) of their children's organs or other tissues. This bond can be conflictual in nature. The conflict begins with the decision the parent is asked to make: While the parent is yet incapable of contemplating the idea of her child's death, she has to make an immediate life-or-death decision about a stranger's needs. The immediacy of this decision triggers an acute grief reaction. Grief, in this case, is neither delayed nor postponed. The parent is confronted with this new reality instantly.

Thus I can relate to most of what Worden (1991) described—except the delayed grief reaction. My grief was not delayed, although for years after Gili's death (and Norm's) I was involved in painful legal procedures. In fact, because an autopsy had to be performed on Gili, my agony was intensified; I also had to decide immediately about organ donation.

For some parents, making such a decision is an additional traumatic experience, which they may re-live in nightmares and intrusive thoughts. Some are plagued with doubts and anxieties, some perhaps unrealistic. For example: What does "braindead" really mean when my child's heart is still beating? Would she feel pain when they cut out her heart? What if she would not have wanted me to make that decision? What will happen to her soul in a mutilated body? (parents may have religious/spiritual beliefs pertaining to such an issue). Later on, when the parents are informed that a recipient has received their child's organs, many parents want to know about the recipient. Although the recipient's identity is kept confidential, some information (gender, age, occupation) is usually disclosed. From that moment on a new process begins to emerge—an *expanded bond* between parent and child through the recipient. It appears that any part of the child symbolizes, to the parent, the whole child. Every surviving cell of the deceased child represents, on some level (spiritual perhaps), the survival of the child. If the recipient survives, it means that the child goes on living, too; if not, the parent experiences yet another loss, as if the child dies again. On one hand, the parent is pleased that the recipient survives (for the recipient's sake, and for the child who continues living through him or her), but on the other hand, the parent may feel resentment toward the recipient, as if the child "had" to die to "provide" this other person with an organ necessary to survival. If the recipient dies, the parent may feel guilt and shame, in addition to that felt for failing to protect/save their child. Or the parent may feel rejected—another form of loss—if the recipient does not respond when the parent attempts contact (through the organ donation organization). Tissue donor parents may grieve differently than organ donor parents. Some parents may be tormented by unanswered questions (e.g., can the recipient "feel" their child?).

*   *   *

"Gili is braindead," said the neurosurgeon. His words will echo in my ears for the rest of my life. He asked me which one of your organs I might be willing to donate. In the initial state of shock, numbness, and some detachment from reality, I had to make a horrendous decision—perhaps only in such a state could I have made such a decision: "Take Gili's heart. She has a good heart." Gili gave in life, and she was going to give in death, I thought. It felt just right. But then I had to live with my decision and with my nightmares. Your heart was still beating but your brain showed no activity anymore. It made me think about the difference between "mind" and "brain." Was it your brilliant mind that had survived physical death and only your brain, that physical organ, that had died? And since your heart was still beating (you looked so much alive, only sleeping, with a tube running out of your pouting lips and a big bandage covering you head), I wondered: Would you feel the pain of harvesting your heart? ("Harvesting!"—the visual image evoked by this new usage of the familiar word slashed suddenly through my internal scream.) And more questions: Who will get your heart? Much later, I was told that it was a 57-year-old judge from Texas who had received your heart, as a second heart to support his ailing one. Through the organ donation organization, I wrote to the judge and enclosed your picture in my letter. But I never received any response, never found out whether the judge is still alive. Not receiving any response from the judge, and not knowing whether he is alive or not, was another death for me. I identified with the parent who once said to me: "My child's life goes on, through the people that the recipient touches throughout her life."

Claire Sylvia (1997), who was a heart and lung recipient, writes that she noticed dramatic changes in her behavior, taste in food, and general outlook on life following the transplant surgery. She also interviewed other organ and tissue recipients, and they all told similar stories. Moreover, most of the recipients also experienced or continue to experience a presence in them. Some have had explicit dreams of what appears to be the donor. Whichever way we may interpret these stories, we reach one conclusion: The parent's continuing bond with the deceased child is profound and is further compounded by the experience of organ/tissue donation.

PHYSIOLOGICAL REACTIONS TO LOSS

When I discovered about 6 years after Gili's death and less than a year after Norm's death that I had a cancerous tumor in my colon (in my "guts"), I felt a sense of relief: What an easy way "out," I thought. I did not want to die; but I desperately wanted to be with Gili and even to visit with Norm. I was not that "lucky," however. I did not conform to the statistics quoted in a popular magazine (which I probably read while sitting in some waiting room) that the average length of life for a bereaved parent after their child dies is 5 years. But because I was already immersed in the development of my theoretical model of parental bereavement and because of my professional background, I was quite versed in neurophysiological and psychoimmunological research (the combined studies of psychology and immunology, or the effect of psychological factors on the immune system). I started searching for some hints that might explain the effect of traumatic loss on the development of illnesses. I also wanted to know whether the physiological changes that take place during grieving are reversible or not. In reviewing the literature, I found that neurophysiological responses to trauma occur at all ages: from childhood through old age. However, the strength of these neurophysiological responses may vary as a function of age; during middle age, for example, the brain decreases its neurological response to anxiety (Bootzin & Acocella, 1984). I wonder if this might explain why I now feel almost a lack of anxiety about major life events, such as illness. I think of my low anxiety level in terms of "the worst has happened to me already," but perhaps it is the decreasing level of norepinephrine in my brain that causes that feeling.

Stress and Disease

Studies of post-traumatic stress disorder resulting from sexual abuse, childhood trauma, homicide, and other sources of distress have clearly demonstrated that neurological and physiological changes occur as a result of trauma and stress, especially when the stress is prolonged. This idea is not new. In 1927, Cannon coined the phrase "fight or flight" to describe the physiological reaction to perceived danger, recognizing that stress and trauma have the potential for evoking a neurophysiological response. These responses occur at three levels: the autonomic nervous system; the neuroendocrine axis, which controls the secretion of adrenaline; and the endocrine axis, which controls the immune system (Friedman, Mason, & Hamburg, 1963).

Kolb (1987), in a study of Vietnam veterans, some of whom were diagnosed with post-traumatic stress disorder, examined the body's neurophysiological response to stress. In response to trauma, Kolb said, the body learns a new way of functioning: When the individual processes intense aversive memories, the body responds with a new or changed neurophysiological protocol.

Some studies on the physiological responses to stress, trauma, and bereavement indicate that individuals who have recently lost a spouse tend to suffer problems with their immune system (Bartrop, Luckhurst, Lazarus, Kiloh, & Penny, 1994; Pettingale, Hussein, & Tee, 1994; Zisook et al., 1994). In discussing behaviorally linked changes in immunity and predisposition to illness, Zakowski, Hall, & Baum (1992) identified bereavement as a potential risk factor in stress-related disease.

Certain psychological characteristics are correlated with susceptibility to cancer (Bootzin & Acocella, 1984). Emotional restraint ("bolting up" strong feelings, either positive or negative), a sense of helplessness or hopelessness, loss of an important personal relationship, and serious life changes are considered possible contributors to the course of cancer by draining the strength of the immune system. There may also be a significant relation between death of a loved one and the development and severity of breast disease in women (Cooper, Cooper, & Faragher, 1989).

The symptoms of temporal lobe epilepsy are similar to the symptoms sometimes present during bereavement. These symptoms include exaggerated emotions, religiosity or a search for spiritual answers, and increased attention to details. Can we assume, then, that in the process of bereavement, particularly at the beginning or during times when the suffering is more acute, there are changes in the limbic system that affect emotions and behavior? Are these changes temporary or of a more permanent nature?

Susceptibility

There isn't a final answer yet. The existing research on different neurophysiological responses to different types of trauma is limited. Everly (1989) attempted to identify the operating process when the same or similar stressors correlate with different target-organ disease. For example, two individuals experiencing similar life stressors may develop different illnesses: One may suffer cardiovascular problems and the other may develop gastrointestinal problems. We do not yet know exactly what determines which stress response. Everly acknowledged the importance of the psychosocial environment, lifestyle, and attitudes in the onset of disease but declined to hypothesize about a direct link or a causal relationship between them. Koolhaas (1994) hypothesized that different coping strategies may account for some of the individual differences found in susceptibility to "stress pathology." According to this model, both active and passive coping styles lead to cardiovascular problems. Specifically, active coping strategies appear to lead to an increased vulnerability to hypertension and atherosclerosis, while passive coping styles may lead to increased vulnerability to cardiac disorders. The nature of the trauma also contributes to the physiological symptoms. For example, a certain type of sexual abuse may result in digestive disorders, including anorexia. Trauma involving hearing, seeing, and talking can result in "hysterical" blindness or deafness, or in elective mutism. Clinical observations suggest that neurophysiological changes due to trauma are largely reversible, especially in children (Armsworth & Holaday, 1993; Everly, 1989; Friedman et al., 1963; Gilliland & James, 1993; Kolb, 1987; Perry, 1992, 1994; Rando, 1994). But can we assume that the more prolonged the trauma, the more neurological pathways are formed, thus "programming" the bereaved child or even the adult to respond in certain ways to similar stimuli? What would be the implications for the treatment of children and adults who have suffered multiple losses? Would it be possible one day to identify the unique neurological, physiological, and biochemical makeup of different types of loss, thus providing us with insights into the different psychological processes of different types of bereavement?

These readings left me with more questions than answers, but this is the nature of most scientific inquiry. Nevertheless, it stimulated me to speculate that different types of parental bereavement (e.g., a stillborn child vs. the death of a child in a car crash) probably involve not only unique psychological processes (unique to that particular type of loss) but also unique physiological and biochemical components.

CHAPTER 7

The Emergence of a New Model:
Parental Grief as a Normal Response

The journey I have made—painful and enlightening—through the words of others about grief gradually led to the realization that some apparently well-accepted notions in the literature are simply neither congruent with my own experience as a bereaved parent nor helpful in my counseling of grief-stricken parents. Over time, these points of disparity have crystallized into alternative interpretations of two major concepts, especially as applied to bereaved parents: the "pathology" of grief, including the survivor's attachment to the deceased child, and the elusive characteristic of resilience so necessary to the survival of the bereaved.

THE QUESTION OF PATHOLOGY

Medical models tend to suggest that disordered affect is almost identical to bereavement: that there is a fine line—sometimes only of magnitude—separating the symptoms of certain pathological conditions from those of bereavement. Freud described melancholy as a distorted grief reaction. Similarly, Naveh (1993) saw melancholy as the pathological reaction of a neurotic personality to a similar event that causes grief in a person with a different personality structure. In comparing grief to depression, Worden (1991) noted that bereaved and depressed clients suffer similar symptoms, including sleep and appetite disturbances, and feelings of sadness. He concluded that a major depressive episode accompanies bereavement. Rando (1993) also noted similarities between grief and depression, and claimed that grief should be diagnosed as separation anxiety.

An interesting study of elderly widows (Prigerson, Frank, & Kasl, 1995) distinguished between bereavement-related depression and *complicated grief*: a separate condition characterized by searching, yearning, preoccupation with thoughts of the deceased, crying, disbelief, feeling stunned, and lack of acceptance of the death. Complicated grief, so defined, was found to be significantly related to impaired global functioning, mood and sleep disturbance, and lowered self-esteem. Although the distinction between complicated grief and bereavement-related depression is helpful in terms of differential diagnosis, the vague definition of terms such as *acceptance* and the assumption that complicated grief leads to less than adequate functioning still tend to pathologize the mourning process.

Deep Sadness Versus Depression

There is a confusion in the bereavement literature between grief as a healthy reaction to loss and depression as an illness; that is, those who view bereavement from a medical perspective often treat parental grief as if it were a form of depression. Whether grief is defined as reactive depression or separation anxiety, it is not recognized for its unique characteristics. Stroebe (1993) noted this tendency to confuse the process of mourning with symptoms of an illness and questioned the assumption that "grief work" is necessary for adjustment to bereavement.

I claim that bereavement is different from depression and that parents' bereavement is different yet from other types of bereavement. Bereavement is a healthy reaction to loss. A better understanding of the different types of mourning, and of depression related and unrelated to bereavement, will enable the provision of more adequate and sensitive help for bereaved parents.

How many times was I told that I was depressed? Even professionals in my field, as well as other people who hardly knew me, suggested that I take antidepressant drugs. And they did so only a short time after Gili was killed. Bereavement is a set of complex reactions often confused with depression. As a result, the bereaved are frequently misunderstood by those around them and too often are mistreated by professionals.

Depression is a mood disorder, probably the most prevalent one, and as such it is widely studied and clinically treated. Depression may, of course, be experienced by nonbereaved individuals, and it is often a chronic condition. When it occurs in conjunction with bereavement, depression may already have existed before the loss occurred. Culbertson (1997), in his international review on gender and depression, revealed that in the last 30 years in the United States and abroad, women have been diagnosed with depression about two or three times more often than have men. Although comparable studies of bereaved parents are needed, I doubt that a similar phenomenon exists among bereaved parents. It is my impression, based on my observations of clients, that there are no gender differences in regard to the experience of *grief*.

I found some support for my view in the literature. Schneider, for example, in *Finding My Way* (1994), made a distinction between grief and depression. These two states, he wrote, vary from each other on issues such as loss; cognitive schemas; dreams and fantasies; physical, spiritual, and emotional states; responses; and pleasure and attachment behavior. Regarding cognitive schemas, for instance, Schneider stated that the difference between grief and depression is that in grieving the person focuses on the loss—the parent thinks about the child all the time and what the loss of that child means to the parent and to that parent's future—while in depression, the person focuses on the self, especially on a distorted and negative self. Or, to take another example, Schneider found a difference in the responses of grieving and depressed individuals. The grieving person responds to warmth, touch, and reassurance; the depressed person, on the other hand, is either unresponsive or responds to promises and urging.

I suggest the use of *deep sadness*—a term specific to grief, particularly parental grief—rather than the erroneous use of the term *depression*. Deep sadness is the constellation of emotions, cognitions, and behaviors characteristic to a parent who has lost a child. I assume deep sadness may characterize other grief processes as well (including children's mourning for their parents), but I know that it is a prominent aspect of parental bereavement.

There are some similarities, but also many differences, between deep sadness and depression. For example, the cause of depression is not always known, and the depression may disappear with or without treatment. With deep sadness, on the other hand, the cause is clear. And although the deep sadness may vary in degree of intensity, it lasts a lifetime and may never turn into depression. I believe that not only the psychological, emotional, spiritual, and cognitive processes but also the physiological, neurological, and biochemical processes involved in depression and deep sadness are different. Deep sadness is similar to the nonclinical condition described in the fourth edition of the *Diagnostic and Statistical Manual of Mental Disorders* (American Psychiatric Association, 1994), better known as *DSM-IV*, as "Non-Complicated Bereavement." Deep sadness, more than depression, is characterized by a spiritual quest and search for meaning. In this search, the bereaved usually finds hope and reason to live, which is not usually the case with the person who suffers from depression.

*   *   *

The Chassidut (Jewish mysticism) distinguishes between *sadness* and *bitterness* in bereavement. Sadness is negative and should not be encouraged because it pulls the bereaved down into depression—and depression is negative because it leads to self-centeredness and detachment from the community. Bitterness, on the other hand, is positive because it motivates the bereaved to move, to act upon their feelings, and to get out into the world. It sounds so different from what we usually hear. Usually the bereaved are encouraged not to become bitter. I even heard myself saying a few times that I am "working to not deepen my bitterness." Like most people, I sometimes confuse bitterness with anger. While bitterness might be one facet of anger, it carries less destructive potential, I think, than anger to act against oneself and others. During Shiva, I believe I heard Gili telling me not to be angry. I did not hear her telling me not to be bitter.

*   *   *

The distinction between deep sadness and depression raises the issue of pathology. "Complicated mourning" and "post-traumatic stress-disorder" need to be better understood for the purpose of assessment and treatment of bereaved parents.

Complicated Mourning. As I mentioned before, the medical models conceptualize mourning as a process progressing toward recovery. Therefore there is "successful recovery" and "unsuccessful recovery." Successful recovery from bereavement is defined by Staudacher (1991) as working through the loss so that one is free from grief-related disturbances. Unsuccessful recovery, on the other hand—also called "pathological grief," "bad mourning," and "unresolved grief"—is defined by such writers as Lindemann (1944), who actually coined the term "pathological grief reaction," as a situation wherein there has been some disturbance in the normal progression toward resolution (see also Hundley, 1993; Rando, 1984, 1993).

Complicated grief takes many forms: absent grief, inhibited grief, delayed grief, conflicted grief, chronic grief, exaggerated grief, masked grief, unanticipated grief, and abbreviated grief. Rando (1993) listed 13 clinical indicators of what she referred to as complicated mourning and 12 symptoms misconstrued as complicated mourning. Among the commonly misinterpreted symptoms are the following: (1) unusually high death anxiety, (2) excessive or persistent overidealization of the deceased, (3) persistent thoughts about the deceased, and (4) an inability to articulate feelings and thoughts about the deceased. However, she also cited Raphael's (1983) caution that we need to examine the validity of the manner in which pathology in mourning is conceptualized. In other words, it is unclear what "complicated mourning" is.

My belief is that parental bereavement is profound and "complicated" by its very nature; that is, parental grief reactions are "excessive," "exaggerated," and lifelong—with unpredictable emotional "spikes" and "valleys." These types of reactions should be expected; they are healthy and, therefore, normal. What may be considered "abnormal" in other circumstances (i.e., obsessive thoughts or preoccupation with a person) is normal for bereaved parents.

Is "absent grief" really the lack of a grief reaction in the bereaved parent? Or does the parent merely have the appearance to an outside observer of not grieving while he or she is grieving internally? Is the ability to mourn inborn, as I claim? I think that we have to understand the experience of grief in light of each individual's social-cultural-spiritual context and not expect parental grief to wear the same face as other kinds of grief.

Post-Traumatic Stress Disorder. Another condition that must be distinguished from bereavement is post-traumatic stress disorder (PTSD). Full-blown PTSD is an anxiety disorder that develops after a traumatic event, an out-of-the-ordinary event, such as the sudden death of a child. Typical characteristics are involuntary flashbacks of the traumatizing event, rage, anger, shock, depleted self-esteem, somatic complaints, startle reactions, and a sense of helplessness. A normal acute grief reaction is a form of PTSD. But after the acute reaction has passed, the process of parental bereavement should not be described as a disorder. There are other differences between PTSD and deep sadness or a parental grief reaction: The grieving parent *wants* to remember and *wants* to be asked about the deceased child and about what he or she is going through; the victim of a trauma does not want to remember or to talk about the experience. In PTSD there might be an *immediate* avoidance reaction to the site where the trauma occurred; in parental grief, there might be a delayed avoidance reaction. I anesthetized myself by passing by the place where Gili was killed and looking at it every single day for several years. Five and a half years later, I moved to another place, but still nearby. I try to avoid driving by Gili's schools.

A PTSD assessment is needed prior to the treatment of parental bereavement in order to rule out the existence of a disorder, a compounding factor in treatment. However, it is important to remember that we must treat with caution any attempt to draw conclusions and make generalizations from studies in related fields. For example, findings of PTSD studies of Vietnam veterans, or studies of traumatized adults who were subjected in their childhood to sexual abuse, should not be applied to the assessment or treatment of adults traumatized by the death of their children.

Attachment/Identification and the New Self

Some writers believe that the bereaved have to relinquish their attachment to the deceased in order to resolve their grief (Sanders, 1986; Volkan, 1983). Failure to do so implies that their grief reaction is pathological. This model views the mourner in relatively passive terms. By contrast, Attig (1996) describes the grieving process as dynamic, as one in which the bereaved is actively involved in making choices about his or her own life. This process requires the learning of new coping skills and an active adjustment to the new reality.

Other researchers acknowledge the fact that continuing the attachment to the deceased is a *normal* grief reaction and that the ongoing relationship is dynamic and changes during the lifespan (Hogan & DeSantis, 1992; Klass et al., 1996; McClowry, Davies, May, Kalenkamp, & Martison, 1995; Stroebe, Stroebe, & Hansson, 1994; Worden & Monahan, 1993). These lines of research normalize the grief response and advocate a more open and flexible conceptualization of bereavement. Some writers incorporate spirituality and the search for meaning in addition to psychological and physiological responses (e.g., Becvar, 1997; Sanders, 1992). This kind of approach conceptualizes attachment with the deceased as an ongoing bond and grief as a lifelong processes.

*   *   *

A phenomenon I have observed in myself is of *"becoming Gili."* It appeared almost as regressive behavior, but it had nothing to do with clinical regression. It had to do with the *emergence of a new self* that incorporated Gili's. My voice became softer and meeker, resembling the voice of a young, insecure child. Part of the phenomenon stemmed from my identification with her personality and my internalization of her mannerisms, I'm sure. I could not have a sexual relationship with Norm, not only because I felt ashamed of being physically alive yet dead inside but also because my internalized 11-year-old baby did not have sex yet.

I started touching things so lightly, feather-like, just like Gili used to do, and I read every book she had in her library: searching for her, yearning to touch what she had touched and to be touched by what had touched her. It took me about 4 years to begin to re-establish my new, composed identity. I observed similar behaviors on my part after Norm's death. I became more outgoing and assertive, at least for a while.

I have noticed this phenomenon in other bereaved mothers as well. It is probable that many of the behaviors seen in bereaved parents are a result of their identification with their children. I think, judging from my own experience, that it is a necessary step inward in order to reconstruct an identity of self. This emerging identity will include aspects of the parent's old self and of the child. This may explain why I used to say that I had a sense that my old self died with Gili and that a new self had started to emerge. I was no active mother to a young child anymore, I was no wife, and I was no university professor. Family and friends left me. Who was I? But once I realized that what was happening was allowing me to incorporate some aspects of Gili's personality, and later Norm's, into my own, then my confusion ended. I did not need the external world anymore to define myself by. I knew who I was. It was then that my views about life and death started to expand. I started to define my life as "before" (Gili's death) and "after."

*   *   *

Klass (1993) wrote that there is no "recovery" in parental mourning and that severing the bond with the dead child does not lead to healthy readjustment or "resolution," adding that severing bonds with the deceased does not stand the test of cross-cultural or of comparative historical analysis. I agree: The idea of detachment is not applicable to the unique case of parental bereavement.

Bereaved parents are different from other types of mourners. The bond between parents and their children is profoundly different from any other relationships that these parents may have. Parents who are mentally healthy are usually attached to their offspring. To expect these parents to detach themselves from the child who has died is an unrealistic and damaging expectation. Bereavement is a process, and it has a goal. The goal is readjustment. The expectation for a "healthy" and "normal" course of readjustment to the loss of the child should include a continuing relationship with that child, though in a transformed manner. In other words, bereaved parents will learn to incorporate the continuing attachment to their child as an integral part of their process of readjustment to a life without the physical presence of their child. Tamir (1993), in an article about the long-term adjustment of Israeli bereaved parents who lost adult sons in wars, stated that the idea of detachment from the object of love, which originated in Freud's concept of decathexis, was not supported by his findings. He concluded that the experience of loss becomes a permanent feeling that accompanies bereaved parents in all aspects of their emotional lives; in the long run, a successful resolution to parental grief is achieved when the parents learn to integrate their sons' images into their emotional and daily lives.

A significant percentage of bereaved parents, even 10 years after their sons were killed in the Yom Kippur War, experienced difficulties in carrying out their responsibilities as family and society members (Florian, 1987); 64% of those parents continued visiting their sons' graves at least once a week (Rubin, 1993).

As I stressed before, bereaved parents never stop grieving as long as they live. And as the Israeli researchers concluded, on a personal level the "flag is at half-mast" every day, while on a societal level it's at half-mast only once a year.

RESILIENCY: LIVING VERSUS SURVIVING

Resiliency consists of both surviving and living. Kfir and Slevin (1993), in their book on cancer survivors, wrote that although people face many dangers in their lives, they relate to the concept of "survival" only when they are aware of the dangers and have to make conscious efforts to overcome or to cope with and to live beyond these dangers. Resilient individuals are characterized by openness, alertness, involvement, and a desire to learn for the sake of learning. The resilient person lives at peace with him- or herself and his or her environment.

Resiliency in relation to parental bereavement means: What does it take to learn to live, not just to survive the death of my child? How can I find meaning in my life, so that my physical survival turns into living, both mentally and spiritually? What lets parents live, and not just survive, after their child dies?

There are many factors involved, including the strength of the pre-loss personality. In other words, what happens to parents after their child dies depends largely on what happened to them *before* their child died. It has been my observation that parents who have suffered major losses in the past, even those who eventually begin living again instead of just surviving, generally experience greater pain and exhibit more severe psychological and physiological reactions for longer periods of time than do those who have not suffered previous losses. I think that what happens to these parents is that the previous losses generally produce a cumulative effect characterized by lack of hope, depletion of life energy, and lowered resiliency for living; the existing resiliency is mainly for physical survival.

However, there are exceptions. Parents who have suffered multiple losses in the past may perceive the death of their child as the most devastating blow, as a sign that there must be some meaning or reason for their continued suffering. This new realization may energize them to begin an inward and outward search for a greater spiritual meaning to their survival. Ultimately, these parents may find hope and meaningful life missions. Sometimes it takes an additional crisis or a life-threatening situation to awaken grieving parents to their inner strength. Becvar (1996), in her article about surviving breast cancer, tells the reader that after the sudden death of her 22-year-old son in an accident, she had given up on life. Later on, she writes "the threat of a terminal illness 'woke me up,' and in the moment of awareness, I made an extremely crucial decision. I verbally affirmed to my husband my commitment to life and living" (p. 87).

The factor called *resilience* is not only physical; it is also emotional and spiritual in nature. When parents survive a loss, they exhibit some form of resiliency. Physical resiliency enables the individual to survive, while emotional and spiritual resiliency empower the individual to live. In general, positive life experiences create a reservoir of hope and inner strength, enabling the afflicted individual to cope better in the aftermath of a traumatic event. A "happy" life usually means sound health, satisfying family and social lives, and a general sense of well-being. Sometimes the person may feel "blessed," especially if he or she has strong spiritual or religious beliefs. As one bereaved mother told me shortly after her 19-year-old son died of cancer, "bad things always happened to other people, not to me. Not to my family."

But there are exceptions. Sometimes a person who generally has not suffered any blows does not cope as well as a person who has lived a less fortunate life. The reasons for this might depend on that *individual's perception, meaning, and interpretation of life events*—the "stories," as Becvar calls them, that they tell themselves about their lives. We might ask: Can the traumatized individual find meaning in the trauma? Can the survivor find a mission or learn a lesson in order to achieve a higher goal? If he can, then the trauma becomes an empowering experience. If she cannot, then it becomes a debilitating experience. And as difficult as it is for me to acknowledge that my tragedy has a purpose, my search for a meaning to my suffering led me to a similar conclusion.

It is common knowledge that bereaved persons cope better if they are supported by family, friends, and their environment in general, leading many persons to believe that external positive support is a necessity for survival and successful coping with the loss. However, even when external support is minimal or when family, friends and colleagues withdraw their support, there are nevertheless some individuals who, in the face of such adversity, are compelled to search for inner resources of coping. In my case, the realization that I had mainly myself to rely on caused me to uncover my innermost core. And it was "steel," in spite of my wish. This discovery of inner strength enables the parent to make a conscious decision to live and not just to survive. My decision was to live in order to honor Gili's life and fulfill her dreams.

Hope and Mission

I used to think, and occasionally say, that if anything happened to Gili, I would die—I would just drop dead. Gili died. Why didn't I?! God knows I wanted and tried to do so. Why did I survive? After countless agonizing journeys into the vast darkness of my soul, searching for meaning in that indescribable terror, I came to the realization that there must be a higher reason for her death and my survival. Perhaps, I thought, we all have missions to complete in this lifetime. Gili, my child, probably completed her mission in her short life; but I did not. I asked myself: "Is *hope* the same as *mission*?" How can I feel as if I have a mission, and at times even think that I know what my mission is, but at the same time feel no hope for my life?

I cannot agree with what Kübler-Ross (1969) has to say about the persistence of hope through all the stages of mourning: that for some grieving people hope is the feeling that their suffering has meaning, but that for others hope remains a form of denial—temporary but nevertheless needed.

Hope, as I define it in this context, is both an anticipation of a positive outcome and an optimistic attitude about the future. I think that perhaps in a state of anticipatory grief, when we know that the ill person is going to die, both the dying person and those who are grieving for that person may feel hope while at the same time experiencing grief. But once the person dies, hope "dies" too. *Hope* is neither experienced throughout the entire process of bereavement, whether or not it progresses through stages or simultaneous steps, nor is it a result of denial, which implies that feeling hope is pathological. I suggest that it might be a sense of *mission*, not hope, that the bereaved parent may experience at first.

But not everyone has a sense of mission and not everyone feels hope. I think that grieving is an inborn reaction to loss. Even animals grieve. But for humans, I think that grieving is the result of the consciousness of having no, or only minimal, control over life events and the results of those events. Following a catastrophic event, people may leap to the conclusion that they have a mission to complete or they may develop a sense of mission gradually.

It has been my observation that the concepts of hope and mission, although interrelated, do not depend on each other. *Hope* implies a sense of optimism—but of passivity, too. It is a realistic conclusion about life events, not an unrealistic or pathological one. *Mission*, on the other hand, does not have to be accompanied by a sense of optimism or even by a sense of accomplishment and success. Sometimes it may even contradict success and hope; for instance, "nothing good can happen, I may even fail, but let me go out and try it anyway." It is felt more as a sense of duty, or a reason for living. It is also, however, a dynamic term that implies activity and goal orientation. The search for hope is almost like a physiological reflex required for survival. From the lack of hope that characterizes the initial reactions after a child's death—from that inability to comprehend why it happened—the bereaved may leap to the conclusion that they have missions to fulfill and, at the same time, rediscover that although they may never find out why this horror has happened, they do have some control over life events and over some of the results of those events, thus finding hope for survival and fulfillment of their mission. There is no timetable according to which these realizations occur.

One mother told me that she started feeling hope again 2 years after her son's death, but only a year after that could she bring herself to look for a new job. In order to survive, I had to redefine my life. I had to reach a new understanding of life, death, after-death, and rebirth. I had to find a new mission. Every choice I made had to fulfill both of our missions, Gili's and mine. And, actually, Norm's too. He asked me on his deathbed to continue his life-work.

This sense of *mission*, which I started to feel shortly after Gili was killed, enabled me to take full responsibility for my feelings, thoughts, and actions. At that time, I started writing about my experiences and resigned a job that had lost its meaning. I have begun to feel *hope*, however, only lately, about 6 years after Gili's death and 2 years after Norm's. With my growing sense of hope and conviction in my mission, I can see at times how my acts of grieving also release my creativity. I feel an increasing need to touch again and to be touched. "And to let the magic take place," as Norm used to say.

CHAPTER 8

The Readjustment Model of Parental Bereavement: Inward and Outward Steps

In Chapters 5–7, I have discussed such topics as hope and mission, deep sadness, and resiliency. I have concluded, after a journey through the literature, that general models of bereavement fail to explain parents' bereavement; that the loss of a child is the most devastating loss any parent can experience; and that parental bereavement is qualitatively different from any other type of bereavement. In this chapter, then, I offer my own interpretation of the process of parental bereavement: the *readjustment model of parental bereavement: inward and outward steps*.

WHAT IS READJUSTMENT?

I reject the idea of a resolution to parental grief. Resolution implies a conscious decision to end grieving. Even if some parents make a decision to end their grieving, I do not believe that they can achieve such a state: the end of mourning. I have not observed in my practice, nor did I experience personally, that there is an end to parental grief. There is no end to the suffering inflicted by the death of one's child. *Resolution* has been defined as a dynamic, ongoing process that continues beyond adaptation and/or coping with loss (Rubin, 1993); nevertheless, when this term is used in the context of bereavement, it usually implies not an ongoing process but rather moving toward the end of the process. Hence my preference for the term *readjustment* rather than *resolution* to describe the process.

To illustrate the concept of readjustment, I first need to share my new belief about the purpose of tragedy in a person's life. I want to believe that there is purpose and reason to life events and that, therefore, there is purpose to the tragic events as well. The purpose of my tragedies and inevitable suffering must be to learn what I had not yet learned through other life experiences (even if this "lesson" almost kills me) and to grow emotionally and spiritually. The ultimate goal, as I choose to believe, is to become the best person I can be in this life. Since with Gili's death my old self undoubtedly died, too, a new self had to emerge. From the ashes of the old, a new self has been developing. This new self, or this old-new person, has to relearn life. It is not an adjustment, therefore, of the same self to a different situation, but a readjustment of the new self to a new reality.

Janoff-Bulman (1992) said that most adults adjust well to the traumas they have experienced, usually without treatment—just by relying on their own resources and the help of relatives and friends who confirm their sense of their own value and their assumptions about the world's benevolence and meaningfulness.

I say that *all* survivors readjust. It is only a matter of pace or quality. Finding meaning for living, a new focus, a new awareness of their strengths, or a mission helps in achieving a better quality of readjustment. The process of readjustment is lifelong.

THE PROGRESS OF READJUSTMENT

Clinical observations (Pine & Brauer, 1986; Rando, 1984) suggest that there are no distinct stages of grief, such as those defined by Kübler-Ross (1969). As I have observed, all emotions occur *at once* and are more intensely felt at the beginning of the process of bereavement.

Simultaneity

The phenomenon of all emotions at once is multifaceted and complex. Let me explain. When a person experiences something familiar, something that they have experienced before, that person has a distinct reaction to that event. But if the person experiences something never experienced before, nor even anticipated, then there has been no opportunity to develop a learned reaction to that event. The mind is overwhelmed by this unfamiliar event, and, as a result, a mass of emotional (and physiological) reactions are felt as though they are occurring at once. It is a chaotic reaction to a catastrophic event. It takes time for the mind to recognize all the components of that event, sort them out, and learn to react in a more distinct manner.

In other words, although the initially unfamiliar event—the death of a child—becomes familiar, the initial reaction of experiencing all emotions indistinctly and all at once has been learned. And therefore, in the future, whenever a similar event occurs, the bereaved parents may once again react in a similar manner—they will once again feel all the emotions at once, even though the intensity of these emotions may vary. While at times the grieving parents may feel overwhelmed by one distinct emotion, such as anguish or anger, most of the time they will feel many emotions at the same time. These emotions may vary in intensity and duration. However, even with the passage of time, they sometimes recur unexpectedly and with full-blown intensity.

Finding a Purpose

Finding a new purpose and a mission is what helped in my readjustment to life without Gili, and later without Norm. I believe that in order to fully readjust to the new reality, bereaved parents must first find a reason, a mission, or a new focus; then they may sometimes find hope as well. Finding a mission is part of the emotional growth that grieving parents experience for the rest of their lives.

The *realization* of the death of the child is often achieved not in a gradual or continuous manner, but *all at once*. However, the *awareness* of this new reality (i.e., life without the child) might be achieved gradually. Contrary to stage, phase, or task theories, in which a state such as "acceptance" or "reconciliation" is defined as a final goal for the bereaved to achieve in order to show a healthy or normal adjustment to the loss, I argue that the process of readjustment is lifelong and is not a goal in itself. Readjustment is an ongoing process—progressing through simultaneous steps taken inward and outward—that lasts a lifetime, and its course is determined by the new purpose, or passion for life, that guides the steps one takes.

Taking Inward and Outward Steps

There are two types of motions, or steps, that I have defined according to two dimensions: *intention and action*. Although the parent may or may not be fully aware of all his or her intentions or actions, the steps are defined relative to the bereaved parent, not to the outside world. *Inward steps* originate and are acted on only in reference to one's self. *Outward steps* originate with the self but are intended and taken toward some component of the outside world; they can be intended to reach out to a single observer or to society in general. For example, if a parent reads a book with the intention of discussing it later with someone else, but never acts on that intention, then reading that book remains an inward step in preparation for an outward step. But if this parent actually reaches out to somebody and discusses the book, then this is an outward step—the intention and the action both connect to the outside world.

Although outside observers (including counselors) cannot really identify (only assume) the inward steps, they may ask the parents what they
have been experiencing, thus increasing the parents' awareness of the inward steps, and assist them in achieving balance. The outward steps, on
the other hand, are public steps; they are more likely to be conscious, self-
aware actions. When bereaved parents engage in outward steps, they appear to be doing things, to be moving around, and, in general, to be connecting with their environment.

The inward steps consist of exploration and search of self and encom-
pass a spiritual search, a search for new purpose, and an exploration of
new goals. These inward and private steps can be thoughts and daydreams
as well as actions, and they may be accompanied by intense *states*, such as
numbness, shock, intolerable and acute pain, hostility, extreme fatigue, and
irritability. Typical *behaviors* are screaming, crying for hours at a time, engaging in self-destructive actions, and experiencing an inability to concen-
trate on what is perceived as "irrelevant." The states and behaviors can be
expressed overtly, so that others may observe them, or privately; they are
inward steps because they are experienced within oneself, without reference to others' feelings or perceptions. Inward steps are sometimes characterized by a general feeling of doom and loss of hope—a sense that the
self "shrinks" and wishes to disappear or that the life force has left or been
drained out forever. Sometimes there is a strong and conscious wish to die.
At other times, inward steps may include an urge to know or to understand what has happened and why.

In contrast, the outward steps are characterized by exploration and
application of one's relationships with the outside world. An outward step
is anything that the bereaved parent does with the intention of connecting
with the outside world; for example, going to the grocery store to buy food.
When the parent acknowledges hunger and then acts on it by going to the
store, a significant step has been taken. The intention here is to re-start a
facet of one's relationship with the outside world. If during this trip to the
store the cashier smiles at the parent or asks the polite question—"How
are you today?"—and the parent actually responds, this is yet another
outward step. Many trips to the store may occur without any response, not
even eye contact, a smile, or a greeting. The first response to the cashier's
polite question may occur during the 50th or 500th such visit to the store;
there is no timetable for the grieving parent. However, many repetitions
of this particular outward step will eventually establish a pattern. In the
process of readjusting to life, one has to re-establish many such new patterns of outward behavior, which may have existed quite firmly prior to
the loss. The initial outward steps are distinguishable because they are a

result of conscious decisions made about each step. But after a pattern has been re-established, the individual steps may not be distinguishable any more; there is no need to make a conscious decision about each step. They become automatic. These outward steps are nevertheless a part of the life-long process of readjustment to life with grieving.

From Inward to Outward Steps

Although the inward and outward steps are simultaneous, there is more *focus* on inward steps right after the child's death. This is when the process of readjustment begins, especially the psychological and spiritual aspects of it. Later on, there is greater focus on the outward steps, where, in the process of readjustment, more of the physical, social, and vocational aspects of life are taking place. The bereaved parents may start taking care of their physical and sexual needs, including exercise, diet, and medical care. At this point there is also a re-engagement with life as new relationships are actively sought out and formed. Vocational changes may be made. There is no timetable as to when the shift in focus occurs. Each process is individual. But the motion from inward to outward, and vice versa, continues throughout the entire life.

Despite this overall shift in focus from inward to outward steps, I did not observe that certain emotions were more "typical" of the beginning, middle, or end of the mourning process, as some researchers have proposed (e.g., Kübler-Ross, 1969). And as I said earlier, the entire process of readjustment terminates only with the cessation of the parent's physical life.

Maintaining a Balance

The bereaved parent achieves some balance only when both inward and outward steps are taken. When balance is maintained, it results in an increased energy level and a sensation that the acute pain, which varies in length and intensity, is gradually becoming more tolerable, although it may never entirely disappear. However, during the entire process of readjustment, or during the bereaved parents' entire lives, they will achieve and lose balance again and again. In that respect, the process of readjustment is an evolutionary one—one that continues to evolve and change depending on the type of steps that have been taken, on their duration and quality, and on the effect these steps have on the parent's perception of grief and of himself or herself as grieving.

Parents do not need an anniversary or any other special date to knock them temporarily "out of balance." Practically anything can do that: a child who looks like yours, a voice, a familiar smell, a greeting card that says "I love you," seeing your child's friend or teacher, a song, an article on children, or a television program that recalls your experiences.

*   *   *

Right now I am "out of balance" again . . . August 25 . . . it was Gili's birthday today, and during the last couple of days I have not been able to stop crying. My pain and longing for her are so acute they take my breath away. I feel withdrawal again and wish to be with Gili *now*. I probably stepped more inward than outward and "fell" out of balance. But had I run away from facing my pain by engaging in some superficial distraction, I would have "fallen" out of balance in the other direction. I have to trust my gut feeling and face the pain head-on. If it drowns me, I need to trust that the same life force, or the same energy that dragged me down, will eventually lift me up. It is, after all, *my* life force that is struggling to survive!

*   *   *

The bereaved parent who is engaged in taking inward steps may appear, to the outside observer, to be withdrawn or even catatonic. But the parent himself feels or knows that he had to withdraw in order to divert inward the little mental and physical energy left in him (grieving is very tiring!), so that he can sustain his physical survival. Ultimately the physical survival, of course, will enable the bereaved parent to start his search for meaningful living. It is important for mental health professionals to understand the necessity of this type of withdrawal, without jumping to premature conclusions about the nature of the behavior, and to understand that bereaved parents do not need to be "rescued" from their (temporary) isolation by medication, hospitalization, or forced involvement in social activities.

If I were to offer just three guiding suggestions to mental health professionals working with bereaved parents, they would be these:

1. *Distinguish between depression and deep sadness.* These distinctions are crucial in order to provide the most appropriate help to the bereaved parent.
2. *Avoid suggesting medication for deep sadness.* Medication may mask the grief reactions and hinder the healthy progression of inward and outward steps. The bereaved parent needs to feel the pain; do not attempt to "take it away" from her.
3. *Offer supportive counseling.* Too often, therapists are eager instead to provide analytical interpretations, which imply pathology. Try to help your clients with their necessary readjustment in ways that are congruent with their family situations, cultural background, and spiritual beliefs. And try to help them achieve a deeper level of understanding about the meaning of what has happened (Ivey, 1983).

THE EVOLUTION OF PARENTAL GRIEF:
EMERGENCE OF A CHILD'S DUAL IMAGE

As the many studies I have cited suggest, unique psychological and sociological issues make the death of a child particularly hard to grieve. These
include the loss related to social expectations of the parents—the social roles
and functions that this child played and was expected to play in the future
in his or her family, and in society at large, in addition to the simple unex-
pectedness of a child's dying before a parent. Other sources that may contribute to the parents' suffering are negative or nonsupportive social reactions that enhance their sense of isolation, loss of support from a spouse,
and the need to care for surviving children. Rando (1986b) also pointed
out that the grief of a bereaved mother in particular is often intensified by
her yearning for the sensory experiences that were part of her caregiving
role, especially when the child was young enough to still require help in
attending to physical needs: eating, bathing, dressing, and so on.

During the process of readjustment, the bereaved parent's perception
of what grief is, of him- or herself as grieving, and of the relationship with
the deceased child changes or evolves. This evolution in the concept of grief,
and of grieving, is directly affected by the inward and outward steps. With
every step taken, inward and outward, into exploration of self and toward
re-engagement with the outside world, the perception of what grief is and
the expectations of themselves as mourners continue to change. As a result, their relationships with their deceased children change, too.

Right after the child's death, the parent can see only the devastation
that the loss has brought. Accordingly, the parent perceives grief as all-
consuming and the self as suspended in time. There is no future, only the
present. The parent becomes grief. After a while, however, with increasing the quantity and quality of steps, the parent experiences other significant changes: He or she starts contemplating and fantasizing "what-if"
kinds of thoughts (e.g., What if my child had gotten married—what would
she have looked like as a bride? How would I have felt as the mother of
the bride?), which enable the evolution of a new relationship with the deceased child. This leads to the development of a *dual image* of the deceased
child: one, the *"real image"* of the child, the concrete image that is fixed in
time; the other, a *"shadow image"* or an abstract image of a growing child,
aging with the passage of time. Although Klass's (1988) concept of the
"inner representation" of the deceased child may sound similar, it is different. His definition of "inner representation" combines some aspects of
the "real image" and the "shadow image," but he did not distinguish between these two phenomena. Some parents may not experience a clear distinction between a real image and a shadow image of their child, especially

if they have grandchildren or other young relatives who *look* like their deceased son or daughter. It seems that the physical resemblance of the living relative reduces the fantasies and the "what-if" kind of thinking that are requisites for the evolution of a dual image.

With the real image of the child, the parent has one type of relationship—one that took place in the past, with a real child, and that is evoked by memories. On the other hand, the relationship of the parent with the child's shadow image projects into the future and is characterized by what-if thinking. *Both types of relationships take place and coexist in the present.* Perhaps this is the true meaning of continuing the bond with the deceased child. As the parent continues to readjust, he or she may realize that the loss has provided opportunities for self-expansion and new challenges for living.

Parents' grief resurfaces as they continue to realize, at certain points, that their child would have graduated, married, and so on. Zvi Givoli (1993), an Israeli bereaved father whose 26-year-old daughter was murdered and who wrote an account of his mourning, said that the pain and grief become only worse with time. I can identify with his experience: Gili's birthday has become much more painful with every passing year. Or should I say that with every passing year I learn to identify more colors, hues, and shades of grieving.

Parental bereavement can never be completed; it is lifelong. Because once your child dies, you, the parent, are denied all future developments in your child's life. Not only is your child denied graduation, marriage, having children; you, too, are also denied all of these expected life events. Shapiro (1994) extended this perspective to incorporate the entire family, whose members need to work toward reconstruction of a new family identity in the aftermath of their loved one's death.

*   *   *

Gili's death not only put me into a constant state of *abnormal* crisis (it's not expected that your child will be killed or will die before you); it also robbed me of *normal* life crises. I will never experience the "empty-nest" crisis or the "my-daughter-is-dating-a-guy-I-don't-like" crisis. Sometimes I wonder, as the years go by: 20 years from now, when other mothers have 11-year-old grandchildren, will I feel the same intense attachment to you, Gili, as I feel now? Will I still be able to hear your voice? I already have to rely on my power of imagination, as the memory of your sweet voice fades away. It hurts. Will you become more and more the shadow image and less and less the real image? Do "shadows" age? Even the thought of you as a shadow hurts. Will my perception of you become more abstract than concrete?

UNDERSTANDING THE GRIEF OF PARENTS

The counseling of bereaved parents should not be based on the expectation or goal that these clients can achieve a state of peace, or even that they should aspire to such a state. With a treatment goal of this sort, intense emotions, attitudes, and behaviors tend to be viewed as pathological; and the intention of the counselor or therapist is to eliminate or at least lessen them.

Instead, I urge grief counselors to consider first the parents' history, their current state of being (intellectual and spiritual, as well as emotional), their changing perceptions of themselves as mourners and of their grief, and their evolving dual-image relationship with their deceased children. Only with this kind of understanding can we as counselors be effective in helping clients to readjust to their changed and changing lives, to cope with ongoing internal and external conflicts, and to function with minimal destructive tendencies toward themselves and toward others.

One concept that well illustrates the need to evaluate bereaved parents' mental health in different terms is that of "dissociation." In nonmourners, dissociation is considered a psychotic reaction: a reaction to trauma in which the self, along with its painful memories, is cast out of consciousness. But as Kaufman (1993) has pointed out, dissociative functioning is part of the normal course of mourning. The initial shock that almost all bereaved parents experience when informed about the death of their child is an example of an acute dissociative reaction. A recent study on survivors of trauma (Shilony & Grossman, 1993) found that individuals who in the face of a traumatic event experienced nonamnesic dissociation, or "depersonalization," exhibited fewer and less intense subsequent psychiatric symptoms than individuals who did not have this experience. It is as if distancing oneself from the traumatic event, at least for a while, without really forgetting what happened, enables the development of healthier coping abilities later.

Respecting Negative Emotions

None of the emotions involved in mourning—such as anger, hostility, or sorrow—dissipate or can be resolved entirely, although their intensity and acuteness may wane at times, especially when a similar experience has not recurred. However, many professionals, and even some bereaved parents, believe that intense grief emotions such as bitterness, anger, or hostility are counterproductive—that such emotions inhibit the bereaved from achieving a "healthy" or "normal" end to their grief, since they supposedly signify that the bereaved parents have been "arrested" in their grief work.

The theory is that these emotions may become destructive, either to the bereaved (in the form of depression) or to others. Therefore, these intense emotions must be "resolved," or at least lessened, through medication and / or psychotherapy. In other words, negative emotions need to be eliminated.

This is a misconception. Intense negative emotions do not necessarily turn into self-destructive emotions. Sometimes these intense grief-related emotions turn into positive energy that mobilizes the bereaved parent to move outward, away from mental and physical paralysis and toward reconnection with the outside world. These emotions can be viewed as *progress* in the process of readjustment. Anger, for example, can be interpreted as an expression of passion. And where there is passion, there is hope!

I will never forget one bereaved mother whose 14-year-old son was killed by a drunk driver who did not stop as children were disembarking from a schoolbus. This mother funneled her rage into researching similar accidents and into efforts to change the law regarding schoolbus drivers' responsibilities. She told me numerous times that "everybody" accused her of going insane because of her intense anger. She said: "My anger is what enables me to get up in the morning and face another day without my son. I know I have things to do to vindicate his senseless death. And I could not have done them had I given up my anger!"

The energy of anger can be harnessed into a positive, self-activating force that enables parents to take control of their shattered self-esteem— and the corresponding lack of motivation to "forgive and forget" does not have to become a self-destructive force, as some believe.

Recognizing Readjustment

It is possible for the professional to evaluate the process of readjustment by identifying the steps that the bereaved parents are taking, by examining the changes in the parents' perceptions of themselves and of their grief, and by assessing these to recognize the emergence of a new purpose, mission, or passion.

Since my model of readjustment is a nonlinear one, however, in which the inward and outward steps are taken simultaneously, it can be difficult to assess a parent's progress. Suppose, for example, that a mother describes her activities as follows: "I lament, sitting on a couch for days, re-running in my mind every detail of my child's last moments." To an outside observer she may look paralyzed, almost catatonic, but the "re-runs" in the mother's mind are inward steps she has been taking. She faces the event, sorts out its components so that the indescribable pain will become, in time, more possible to deal with. But while she is sitting on the couch, she may reach out to pick up a book recommended by a friend, resolving to read and share her reactions. Or she may respond to a telephone call. These are outward steps, reconnecting her to the outside world. This mother has been doing the "grief work," taking both inward and outward steps.

FACTORS TO EXPLORE IN TREATMENT

When trying to help bereaved parents, counselors and therapists need to take into consideration many factors. The exploration of these can significantly contribute to the understanding of the bereaved parent's condition in the present and enable the client and counselor to work together more effectively toward a new future. The following list, although not comprehensive, is culled from my work with clients as well as my own experience as a bereaved parent.

1. *The age and history of both parent and child.* Though this may be very basic information, it is surprising how the particularity of each loss can be ignored or minimized by a counselor intent upon helping a client according to a preconceived idea of the grieving process. Every client is different, and every death is an individual loss suffered by a particular survivor. It is important first to understand the parent's view of the loss, which can be gained from an account of the child's life and the parent–child relationship.
2. *The child's personality and relationships with family members and others.* This information enables the counselor to gain a better understanding of the continuing bond of the various family members with the deceased child. In addition, an understanding of the important relationships in the child's life may help the counselor to interpret a parent's feelings of guilt, shame, anger, regret, and despair. Each parent has to cope not only with her loss but also with the feelings of others, both within and outside the family, who were to various degrees attached to her child—and also with the altering of such relationships following the child's death.
3. *The parent's outlook on life before the loss.* This will provide some clues about his abilities to find a new purpose or a new passion in the future—an important factor in helping to improve the quality of the readjustment process. A client's outlook includes reactions to previous losses, which are important as indicators of future resiliency. Such information about the past can help in assessing whether a parent is currently experiencing deep sadness, depression, or post-traumatic stress disorder.
4. *The symbolic meaning of the child's life to the parent.* It is essential that the counselor explore this meaning with the parent in order both to under-

stand the nature and magnitude of the loss and to recognize the emergence of a new self or new identity. Thus an exploration of the child's dreams and aspirations, and the parent's dreams for that child, can help not only in understanding the depth of the parent's despair but also in identifying new goals or missions for the parent.

5. *Cultural factors pertaining to loss; spiritual beliefs and practices; and premonitions.* Information about all of these can provide valuable insights into the process of readjustment. Accounts of premonitions (both the child's and the parent's) can help the counselor gain a better understanding of sources of hope, guilt, or helplessness for the parent. Cultural factors include everything from mourning practices to philosophies about death in general. Cultural expectations often strongly influence a parent's perception of grief and of his or her role as mourner.

6. *Family and social support; employment and financial situation.* Finally, these external conditions are important contributors to the parent's resiliency; their strength and stability affects the parent's ability to survive and find reasons for living.

Grieving should be perceived as a healthy process of readjustment to life with bereavement. Metaphorically, it is a process of rebirth, or of giving birth to a "new self" that only slightly resembles the old. The counselor can be an effective midwife in this birthing process only with a thorough knowledge of the client's history and a clear understanding of what will be life-sustaining for his or her new, reborn self.

POSTLUDE

From Yesterday Toward Tomorrow

All the complexity of human interaction continues beyond life into mourning. The parent continues interacting with the deceased child, although in a metaphorical form. Rituals such as lighting Yahrzeit candles, writing poetry, and keeping or wearing objects that belonged to the deceased have been called "linking objects" (Volkan, 1983). These are either actual objects that belonged to the deceased, and therefore become important to the mourner, or symbolic acts that connect the mourner to the deceased.

"Like the way you display my artwork in your house."

Hey, you're back! I missed you.

"I missed you, too. It was hard to be eavesdropping quietly all that time!"

Feel free to jump in any time, Mommile. Your miniature sculptures, love notes and pictures, the dollhouse that you built together with Norm, your golden bracelet that I wear because your name was inscribed on it—all are linking objects. I perceive the need to hold on permanently or temporarily to linking objects as the need to turn the abstract into the concrete, to turn the metaphysical and untouchable into the physical and touchable.

"Your decision to hold on to 'linking objects' was an example of an inward step, no?"

Yes. And my actual wearing of your bracelet or your earrings is an example of an outward step, because it is a form of communication with the outside world. Each item delivers a message about you, about myself, and about my bond to you.

I cannot hold you in my arms anymore, but I can touch your headstone and I can touch the things you once touched. My need for the concrete and touchable is part of my coping with the finality of your physical absence from my life.

"You visit my grave (and Norm's) once or twice a week."

Yeah. I clean and plant new shrubs and flowers. It is as if I visit your room, to clean and decorate it. It gives me the satisfaction of doing something concrete for you.

"I understand that, Ima. I saw other parents do similar things."

Visiting the gravesite so often is more common in Israel than it is here, in the United States. The memorial libraries that I donated to your two schools and to universities in Israel and in the United States, the scholarships—all are linking objects that symbolize your generous and giving spirit. Also, commemorating you publicly has served as a way to turn my private loss into a societal loss. Thus I acknowledge the importance of your life, and of your death.

I am still your mother. I have a need to talk about you, Gili, to mention your name frequently. This is especially true when people who knew you, or who know that I am a bereaved mother (and a widow), shy away from even mentioning your name or referring to what happened to you. So I make it a daily habit to mention your name and to talk about you whenever I feel like doing so. It soothes my pain a little bit.

People who knew both of you would rather talk to me about Norm than about you.

"Talking about a dead child is more threatening, especially to a parent."

I guess so. Talking about you means acknowledging their own vulnerability and helplessness when it comes to assuring the physical survival of their children or of other children they know. And it might be even larger than that—just acknowledging a child's mortality must be terrifying.

I have observed in myself, and in other bereaved parents, the emergence of an altruistic need to help other bereaved persons. In the process of redefining one's mission, and in the search for a meaningful purpose, there's hope for change. This mission may become the lever that enables the bereaved to identify and recognize their newly emerging life as a challenge, not as an obstacle.

"Mom, there must be pain involved in this new perception of life."

Yes. This is because bereaved parents have to give up, to a certain extent, their own wish to die.

"So you had to acknowledge, first, the life force in yourself."

Exactly. I had to acknowledge that my death wish and my life force can and do coexist; only the life force is getting stronger. The life force becomes the motivator, the cause and the effect all together.

When this process takes place, the general sense of numbness is lifted—not entirely, but for most of the time. In its place a new sensation of excitement emerges, almost as if a miracle, a rebirth of self, has happened. I feel as though you, Gili and Norm, are both smiling at me, as if you are happy with my rebirth.

"Yes, I am smiling at you. And I have a feeling that Norm does the same."

*   *   *

My rebirth culminated almost 5 years after your death and about 4 months after Norm's death, at the end of the summer of 1994. It was the first time since you died that I could think of the future and make plans. It reached a peak by mid-December—the first time that I felt alive again. You may want to know how this happened. How can one move from total devastation toward rebirth, toward a sense of hope and future? My explanation of what transpired, that shift in me, is as follows: The first turning point occurred earlier, when I acknowledged that I had survived your death, that I could not will myself to die, and that I have a mission to fulfill in this life. That mission is to help the bereaved—a combination of your mission and mine. I always felt that I had some mission to fulfill. I just was not focused in my efforts. Now, I knew that we all serve a higher purpose.

The realization that there must be a reason for my survival pushed me to begin what came naturally to me—writing. I promised you to write your life story, so I started writing *Gili's Book*. I felt your guidance all along. It was *our* project. I still keep a journal of your visitations and my dreams about you, and there is much more writing in me. Perhaps, in the process of identification with you and the internalization of aspects of your personality, I adopted your "feverish" writing habit. You used to write as if there was no tomorrow—now I do the same. From the start I intended your story to be published. This writing was my beginning of re-engaging life.

The second turning point happened when Norm was diagnosed with terminal cancer. It was clear from the beginning that he would need help 24 hours a day. He wanted that help from me, and there was no way that I was not going to help him in exactly the way he needed. In one respect my emerging life was interrupted. On the other hand, being needed and the realization that I was going to face another separation—although not as sudden as that from you, Gili, and not as devastating—freed my arrested energy. The physical act of *doing things*, of caring for Norm, released and generated increasing mental and physical strength from a source I had thought was long gone. I see these turning points from total devastation to hope as miracles. Not only was there spirit left in me, but I also experienced with certainty a surge of new vitality. This certainty reinforced me, and as my inner strength increased so did my conviction that my life had meaning. I still have a big job to complete now: mine, yours, and Norm's. I do not know where other bereaved parents and spouses derive their inner strength. Mine seemed to emerge, paradoxically, when I surrendered my own needs to Norm's. In a way, in his dying, Norm gave me the gift of living. He enabled me to love again and to feel loved.

"But what about parents who do not think in terms of 'a mission'?"

These parents still need to acknowledge the life force within them and to find a purpose, a vision, or a new passion for living, not just for surviving. They may decide to do volunteer work with other bereaved parents or to show more compassion to their surviving family members, whatever it takes for them to express their re-connectedness with life. In my case, I had a particularly hard time approaching new people because of the abandonment by family, old friends, and colleagues that I had experienced. But I felt that if I stayed much longer in that forced isolation, there was a risk that I might never regain trust in people again. This could not be an indicator of good mental health, I thought. So I used the excuse of a temporary medical problem and forced myself to exercise in a hotel's swimming pool. I felt safe in the hotel. The pool was heated. Warm water always soothed me. It was noisy enough that my crying was not heard (just in case any of my imaginary audience would have cared enough to watch me and wonder), my tears blended in with the water, and my red eyes could have been attributed to the chlorine (again for my merciless "audience"). I did not have to make eye contact with anybody, but I nevertheless felt as if I were reaching out to the outside world. I did what "normal" people do. In the water I did not look or feel more incapacitated than any other "handicapped" who was swimming along with me. My main "contribution" at that time was to increase the level of saltiness in the water. This was not too harmful, I thought!

I find myself laughing sometimes, and I feel enjoyment at times. Alan, my special friend, has been crucial in assisting me in the readjustment process. I can even relate to children with less pain than before. I have no sense of betraying you or Norm. I feel as though the three of us, together and separately, have started a new life. At the same time I feel as if the outer world is opening up to me, too—people find it easier to respond to me when I'm reacting with less (overt) pain and withdrawal.

"Every day presents you with a new challenge, a new test for survival, doesn't it?"

Yes. Every day confronts me with the ongoing conflict: curiosity about my future but, at the same time, readiness to give up everything, in a heartbeat, just to be with you! I continue to discover depths of suffering that are beyond description.

*   *   *

I believe that in time—when a different perspective about a child's death, about one's self, one's relationships, one's life and death is gained—the deep sadness and all the other emotions described earlier will still exist but at times may be lessened in their intensity or duration.

Or perhaps a greater ability to tolerate the pain emerges. I know that no matter how much time has elapsed, any small event that triggers memories—seeing a picture not seen before, listening to an old recording of your voice, seeing a stranger who resembles you, hearing a child calling "Mommy" or "Ima," seeing a mother and daughter embracing in a long loving hug, finding myself performing a gesture typical to you, meeting one of your former friends—immediately evokes an acute pain, a pain almost as sharp and overwhelming as on the day you died. These are my days, and my nightmares. Once again, all the emotions are felt at once.

Images of you, my heart, lying on your deathbed; you, my child, being put into the ground, the hard winter soil thumping on your coffin—these and many other horrifying images, sounds, and smells haunt me and crush me at unexpected times and when I am least prepared for them.

"But in spite of all this, only when you allow yourself to mourn do you allow yourself to live as well."

I agree. Only when the bereaved acknowledges that "I mourn, I am bereaved" can the process of "living" begin. The trauma may offer an opportunity. From the old life, a new life emerges, a life that encompasses mourning.

*   *   *

Based on my clinical and personal experience, I cannot say often enough that bereaved parents exhibit a wide range of grief reactions. There are those who integrate their grief and mourning into their lives and apparently readjust well to a new life without the physical presence of their child. There are those parents who seem, to the outsider, as if they have been arrested in their grief for a very long period of time; these parents might be immersed in taking inward steps more than outward steps. Other parents have what appears to be a delayed grief reaction; the full acknowledgment of their monumental loss may occur later, when either a neutral event or another loss may trigger the grief reaction for the loss of their child. The lack of immediate, recognizable grief reactions in a bereaved parent—or, in contrast, the seemingly overlong duration of grieving—does not necessarily mean that a pathological process is taking place. Parental bereavement, because of its intensity, is more varied in its manifestations than any other type of bereavement. As I stated before, "good grief" is a matter of circumstances, historical and cultural context, and definitions.

My personal bereavement is an illustration of one individual's grief within a particular historical and cultural context: I am an Israeli Jewess, the child of Holocaust survivors; I grew up in a family and among people who had suffered horrendous losses and, as a result, knew unending mourning, in a country where loss and mourning were and still are an integral part of living. Until the Yom Kippur War, mourning was generally not acknowledged in Israel as an appropriate reaction to a "heroic" death; since then, there has been a significant change in Israeli attitudes toward both death and bereavement, especially war-related death and parental bereavement.

A similar trend is emerging in the United States, as evidenced by the increase in grief-related publications. Perhaps the growing importance of individuality over nationality has caused this change in the perception of grief. Being a product of both the Israeli and American cultures, and living in a social climate that accepts and even encourages public acknowledgment of personal bereavement, I express my emotions and my thoughts publicly.

"In so doing, you also acknowledge and share your vulnerability."

Yes, my overt behavior is part of my mission: I would like to encourage other bereaved parents to share with others their intense emotion rather than keeping it to themselves.

The process of my readjustment to life with mourning demonstrates the inward as well as the outward steps I took and continue to take. My perception of grief and of myself as a bereaved mother continues to evolve and change. In that respect, my model of parental bereavement cannot be completed. Because of its dynamics, it will continue to develop for as long as I live. We should remember that there is no "going back" psychologically, spiritually, physiologically, socially, or cognitively. Bereaved parents should not expect to feel, look, act, think, or relate to others in the same way as they did before their child's death. However, this trauma can also present a chance for a new beginning, as painful as it is, for a new mission to be identified and fulfilled, and for a new or different meaning of life to be found. We, the bereaved parents, can re-learn how to live, not just to survive!

*   *   *

These thoughts help me in my merciless journey from one milestone to another. I think, Gili, that our relationship will continue to evolve in many profound ways as we continue to grow spiritually. And for some strange reason, the thought of it fills me with anticipation and excitement, not just with sorrow. Maybe it is something to look forward to.

Now, I can almost hear your sweet voice urging me gently, "Don't cry, Mommilee sheli. I am fine, really. I am with you, and I am growing, too, in my way. You don't need to feel as if you are becoming an old mother to a young-forever child. And although you will not go to my graduation or to my wedding, you went to my brother's. Remember what Nilli, that little Israeli girl, wrote to you? Something like "Think of her (me) as if she went on a trip. Very soon you'll take the same trip, and think how happy the two of you (us) will be when you meet again!"

Thank you for reminding me which way to turn. Sometimes I lose my compass.

And we will continue loving and talking, my Gili.

"Ani ohevet otach (I love you), Mommy!"

Bibliography

American Psychiatric Association. (1994). *Diagnostic and statistical manual of mental disorders* (4th ed.). Washington, DC: Author.

Argaman Barnea, A. (1996). *Amarti malachim* [Angels, I said]. Tel Aviv, Israel: Bitan.

Armsworth, M. W., & Holaday, M. (1993). The effects of psychological trauma on children and adolescents. *Journal of Counseling & Development, 72,* 49–56.

Attig, T. (1991). The importance of conceiving of grief as an active process. *Death Studies, 15*(4), 385–393.

Attig, T. (1996). *How we grieve.* New York: Oxford University Press.

Baker, J. E., Sedney, M. A., & Gross, E. (1992). Psychological tasks for bereaved children. *American Journal of Orthopsychiatry, 62*(1), 105–116.

Barnes, R. C. (1994). Finding meaning in unavoidable suffering. *International Forum for Logotherapy, 17*(1), 20–26.

Bartrop, R. W., Luckhurst, E., Lazarus, L., Kiloh, L. G., & Penny, R. (1994). Depressed lymphocyte function after bereavement. In A. Steptoe & J. Wardle (Eds.), *Psychosocial processes and health: A reader* (pp. 166–170). Cambridge, England: Cambridge University Press.

Becvar, D. S. (1996). I am a woman first: A message about breast cancer. *Families, Systems & Health, 14*(1), 83–87.

Becvar, D. S. (1997). *Soul healing.* New York: Basic Books.

Bertman, S. L. (1991). *Facing death: Images, insights, and interventions.* Bristol, England: Taylor & Francis.

Bolton, I., & Mitchell C. (1996). *My son, my son.* Atlanta: Bolton.

Bootzin, R. R., & Acocella, J. R. (1984). *Abnormal psychology: Current perspectives.* New York: Random House.

Bowlby, J. (1980). *Attachment and loss: Vol. 3. Loss, sadness and depression.* New York: Basic Books.

Bramblett, J. (1991). *When good-bye is forever: Learning to live again after the loss of a child.* New York: Ballantine.

Braun, M. J., & Berg, D. H. (1994). Meaning reconstruction in the experience of parental bereavement. *Death Studies, 18*(2), 105–129.

Braza, K. (1997). *To touch a grieving heart* [Video]. Salt Lake City: Panacom Video Publishing.

Brende, J. O. (1995). Twelve themes and spiritual steps: A recovery program for survivors of traumatic experiences. In G. S. Everly, Jr. & J. M. Lating (Eds.), *Psychotraumatology: Key papers and core concepts in post-traumatic stress* (pp. 211–229). New York: Plenum.

Buirski, C.K., & Buirski, P. (1994). The therapeutic mobilization of mourning in a young child. *Bulletin of the Menninger Clinic, 58*(3), 339–354.

Chance, S. (1992). *Stronger than death.* New York: Norton.

Chu, J. A. (1992). The therapeutic roller coaster. *Journal of Psychotherapy Practice and Research, 1*(4), 351–354.

Cleiren, M., Diekstra, R., Kerkhof, A. J., & van der Wal, J. (1994). Mode of death and kinship in bereavement: Focusing on "who" rather than "how." *Crisis, 15*(1), 22–36.

Connell, J. P. (1985). A new multidimensional measure of children's perceptions of control. *Child Development, 56,* 1018–1041.

Cooper, C. L., Cooper, R., & Faragher, E. B. (1989). Incidence and perception of psychosocial stress: The relationship with breast cancer. *Psychological Medicine, 19*(2), 3290.

Corr, C. A., Nabe, C. M. & Corr, D. M. (Eds.) (1997). *Death & Dying. Life & Living.* Pacific Grove, CA: Brooks/Cole.

Crider, T. (1996). *Give sorrow words.* Chapel Hill: Algonquin Books of Chapel Hill.

Culbertson, F. M. (1997). Depression and gender: An international review. *American Psychologist, 52*(1), 25–31.

Davies, P. (1996). *Grief: Climb toward understanding.* San Luis Obispo, CA: Sunnybank.

DeSpelder, L. A., & Strickland, A. L. *The last dance: Encountering death and dying.* Mountain View: Mayfield.

de Vries, B., Lana, R. D., & Falck, V. T. (1994). Parental bereavement over the life course: A theoretical intersection and empirical review. *Omega: Journal of Death and Dying, 29*(1), 47–69.

Doka, K. J. (Ed.). (1989). *Disenfranchised grief: Recognizing hidden sorrow.* New York: Lexington Books.

Doka, K. J. (1993). *Living with life-threatening illness.* New York: Lexington Books.

Doka, K. J. (Ed.). (1996). *Living with grief after sudden loss.* Bristol, PA: Taylor & Francis.

Edelstein, L. (1984). *Maternal bereavement.* New York: Praeger.

Everly, G. S. (1989). *A clinical guide to the treatment of the human stress response.* New York: Plenum.

Figley, C. R. (Ed.). (1985). *Trauma and its wake: Vol. I. The study and treatment of post-traumatic stress disorder.* New York: Brunner/Mazel.

Figley, C. R. (1989). *Helping traumatized families.* San Francisco: Jossey-Bass.

Finkbeiner, A. K. (1996). *After the death of a child: Living with loss through the years.* New York: Free Press.

Finkelstein, A. (1985). *Your past lives and the healing process.* New York: Coleman.

Fitzgerald, H. (1994). *The mourning handbook.* New York: Simon & Schuster.

Florian, V. (1987). Meaning and purpose in the lives of bereaved parents. *Chevra Urevacha, Zayin, 3,* 242–252.

Freud, S. (1957). Mourning and melancholia. In J. Strachey (Ed. & Trans.), *The Standard Edition of the complete works of Sigmund Freud* (Vol. 14, pp. 239–258). London: Hogarth Press. (Original work published 1917)

Friedan, B. (1993). *The fountain of age.* New York: Simon & Schuster.

Friedman, S. B., Mason, J. W., & Hamburg, D. A. (1963). Urinary 17–hydroxy-corticosteroid levels in parents of children with neoplastic disease: A study of chronic psychosomatic stress. *Psychosomatic Medicine, 25*, 364–370.

Furman, E. (1974). *A child's parent dies.* New Haven, CT: Yale University Press.

Furman, E. (1984). Children's patterns in mourning the death of a loved one. In H. Wase & C. A. Corr (Eds.), *Childhood and death* (pp. 185–202). Washington, DC: Hemisphere.

Gilliland, B. E., & James, R. K. (1993). *Crisis intervention strategies.* Pacific Grove, CA: Brooks/Cole.

Givoli, Z. (1993). *There is also hope in bereavement.* Jerusalem: Canna.

Gosman, M. (1996). *In the wake of death: Surviving the loss of a child.* Wakefield, RI: Moyer Bell.

Guggenheim, B., & Guggenheim, J. (1996). *Hello from heaven.* New York: Bantam.

Hendel, Y. (1991). *Har hatoim* [The mountain of losses]. Tel Aviv: Hasifriya Hachadasha, Hotzaat Hakibbutz Hameuchad/ Sifrei Siman Kriaa.

Heschel, A. J. (1990). *Quest for God.* New York: Crossroad.

Hobbie, D. (1996). *Being Brett.* New York: Holt.

Hogan, N., & DeSantis, L. (1992). Adolescent sibling bereavement: An ongoing attachment. *Qualitative Health Research, 2*(2), 159–177.

Hundley, M. E. (1993). *Awaken to good mourning.* Arlington, TX: Crocker Associates.

Irish, D. P., Lundquist, K. F., & Nelson, V. J. (Eds.). (1993). *Ethnic variations in dying, death, and grief: Diversity in universality.* Washington, DC: Taylor & Francis.

Ivey, A. (1983). *Intentional interviewing and counseling.* Monterey, CA: Brooks/Cole.

Janoff-Bulman, R. (1992*). Shattered assumptions: Towards a psychology of trauma.* New York: Free Press.

Kaminer, H. (1993). Repression during awakening and sleep—An adjustment mechanism in coping with the traumatic experiences of the Holocaust survivors. In R. Malkinson, S. Rubin, & E. Vitzom (Eds.), *Loss and mourning in the Israeli society* (pp. 71–89). Jerusalem: Cana and Ministry of Defense, publishers.

Kandt, V. E. (1994). Adolescent bereavement: Turning a fragile time into acceptance and peace. *School Counselor, 41*(3), 203–211.

Kaufman, J. (1993). Dissociative functions in the normal mourning process. *Omega: Journal of Death and Dying 28*(1), 31–38.

Kfir, N., & Slevin, M. (1993). *Ma shetalui becha* [Challenging cancer: From chaos to control]. Tel Aviv: Am Oved.

Klass, D. (1988). *Parental grief: Solace and resolution.* New York: Springer.

Klass, D. (1993). Solace and immortality: Bereaved parents' continuing bond with their children. *Death Studies, 17*, 343–368.

Klass, D. (1995). Spiritual aspects of the resolution of grief. In H. Wass & R. Neimeyer (Eds.), *Dying: Facing the facts* (pp. 243–268). Philadelphia: Taylor & Francis.

Klass, D., Silverman, P. R., & Nickman, S. L. (Eds.). (1996*). Continuing bonds. New understandings of grief.* Washington, DC: Taylor & Francis.

Klein, S. J. (1998). *Heavenly hurts. Surviving AIDS–related deaths and losses.* Amityville, CA: Baywood Publishing Company, Inc.

Kolb, L. C. (1987). A neuropsychological hypothesis explaining posttraumatic stress disorder. *American Journal of Psychiatry, 144*(8), 989–995.

Koolhaas, J. M. (1994). Individual coping strategies and vulnerability to stress pathology. *Homeostasis in Health and Disease, 35*(1–2), 24–27.

Kübler-Ross, E. (1969). *On death and dying.* New York: Collier.

Kunen, J. S. (1994). *Reckless disregard.* New York: Simon & Schuster.

Kushner, H. S. (1981). *When bad things happen to good people.* New York: Avon.

Lahad, M., & Ayalon, O. (1995). *Al hachaim veal hamavet* [On life and death]. Tivon, Israel: Nord Publications.

Larson, D. G. (1993). *The helper's journey: Working with people facing grief, loss, and life-threatening illness.* Champaign, IL: Research Press.

Larson, D. G., & Chastain, R. L. (1990). Self-concealment: Conceptualization, measurement and health implications. *Journal of Social and Clinical Psychology, 9*(4), 439–455.

Levinthal, C. F. (1990). *Introduction to physiological psychology.* Englewood Cliffs, NJ: Prentice-Hall, Inc.

Lindemann, G. (1944). Symptomatology and management of acute grief. *American Journal of Psychiatry, 101,* 141–148.

Linn, E. (1990). *150 facts about grieving children.* Incline Village, NV: The Publisher's Mark.

Lord, J. H. (1987). *No time for goodbyes.* Ventura, CA: Pathfinder Publishing.

Lord, J. H., & Mercer, D. (1997, June). *Vehicular crash victims: Grief, depression, posttraumatic stress or brain injury?* Paper presented at the conference of the Association of Death Education and Counseling, Washington, DC.

Malkinson, R., & Viztom, E. (1996). From "Magash hacesef" to "Mi izcor et hazochrim": Psychological aspects of mourning in historical and literaric analyses. *Alpayim—A multidiciplinary publication for contemporary thought and literature.* Tel Aviv: Am Oved.

Martin, J., & Romanowski, P. (1988). *We don't die.* New York: G. P. Putnam's Sons.

Matsakis, A. (1992). *I can't get over it: A handbook for trauma survivors.* New York: New Harbinger Publications.

McClowry, S. G., Davies, E. B., May, K. A., Kulenkamp, E. J., & Martison, I. M. (1995). The empty space phenomenon: The process of grief in the bereaved family. In K. J. Doka (Ed.), *Children mourning, mourning children* (pp. 149–162). Washington, DC: Hospice Foundation of America.

Miles, M. S. (1984). Helping adults mourn the death of a child. In H. Wass & C.A. Corr (Eds.), *Childhood and death* (pp. 219–239). Washington, DC: Hemisphere.

Miller, T. W. (1995). Stress adaptation in children: Theoretical models. *Journal of Contemporary Psychotherapy, 25*(1), 5–14.

Mitchard, J. (1996). *The deep end of the ocean.* New York: Viking.

Mogenson, G. (1959). *Greeting the angels. An imaginal view of the mourning process.* Amityville, NY: Baywood.

Morse, M. (1994). *Parting visions.* New York: HarperCollins.

Moses, S. (1991, January). Children can overcome untimely death of parents. *The APA Monitor,* pp. 6–7.

Naveh, H. (1993). *Beshvi haevel* [Perspectives of mourning in Hebrew literature]. Tel Aviv: Hotzaat Hakibbutz Hameuchad.

Norris, F. H. (1992). Epidemiology of trauma: Frequency and impact of different potentially traumatic events on different demographic groups. *Journal of Consulting and Clinical Psychology, 60*(3), 409–418.

Osho. (1995). *Omanut hamita* [The art of dying]. Herzelyah, Israel: Gal Publishing.

Parkes, C. M. (1985). Bereavement. *British Journal of Psychiatry, 146,* 11–17.

Pendelton, D., & Pendelton, L. (1990). *To dance with angels.* New York: Zebra.

Perry, B. D. (1992). *Neurodevelopment and the psychophysiology of trauma. I: Conceptual considerations for clinical work with maltreated children.* Manuscript submitted for publication, Baylor College of Medicine, Houston, TX.

Perry, B. D. (1994). Neurobiological sequelae of childhood trauma: PTSD in children. In M. Murburg (Ed.), *Catecholamine function in posttraumatic stress disorder: Emerging concepts* (pp. 233–255). Washington, DC: American Psychiatric Press.

Pettingale, K. W., Hussein, M., & Tee, D. E. (1994). Changes in immune status following conjugal bereavement. *Stress Medicine, 10*(3), 145–150.

Pine, V. R., & Brauer, C. (1986). Parental grief: A synthesis of theory, research, and intervention. In T.A. Rando (Ed.), *Parental loss of a child* (pp. 59–97). Champaign, IL: Research Press.

Pfost, K. S., Stevens, M. J., & Wessels, A. B. (1989). Relationship of purpose in life to grief experiences in response to the death of a significant other. *Death Studies, 13*(4), 371–378.

Prigerson, H. G., Frank, E., & Kasl, S. V. (1995). Complicated grief and bereavement-related depression as distinct disorders: Preliminary empirical validation in elderly bereaved spouses. *American Journal of Psychiatry, 152*(1), 22–30.

Puryear, A. (1996). *Stephen lives! My son Stephen: His life, suicide and afterlife.* New York: Pocket Books.

Ragland, C. (1993, January). Ten years after. *Compassionate Friends Newsletter,* pp. 1–2.

Rando, T. A. (1984). *Grief, dying and death.* Champaign, IL: Research Press.

Rando, T. A. (1986a). Parental bereavement: An exception to the general conceptualizations of mourning. In T.A. Rando (Ed.), *Parental loss of a child* (pp. 45–59). Champaign, IL: Research Press.

Rando, T. A. (1986b). The unique issues and impact of the death of a child. In T.A. Rando (Ed.), *Parental loss of a child* (pp. 5–45). Champaign, IL: Research Press.

Rando, T. A. (1988). *How to go on living when someone you love dies.* New York: Bantam.

Rando, T. A. (1992–93). The increasing prevalence of complicated mourning: The onslaught is just beginning. *Omega: Journal of Death and Dying, 26*(1), 43–59.

Rando, T. A. (1993). *Treatment of complicated mourning.* Champaign, IL: Research Press.

Rando, T. A. (1994). Complications in mourning traumatic death. In I. Corless, B. Germino, & M. Pittman (Eds.), *Dying, death, and bereavement: Theoretical perspectives and other ways of knowing.* Boston: Jones & Bartlett.

Rando, T. A. (1996). On treating those bereaved by sudden, unanticipated death. In *Session: Psychotherapy in practice, 2*(4), 59–71.

Rando, T. A., & Figley, C. R. (1996, December). *Trauma and loss*. Paper presented at the Hindle & Associates workshop, Toronto, Canada.

Raphael, B. (1983). *The anatomy of bereavement*. New York: Basic Books.

Rosen, H., & Cohen, H. L. (1981). Children's reactions to sibling loss. *Clinical Social Work Journal, 9*(3), 211–219.

Rosenblum, D. (1997, January 29). The old in one another's arms. *New York Times Magazine*, pp. 52, 62.

Rosof, B. D. (1994). *The worst loss: How families heal from the death of a child*. New York: Holt.

Rubin, S. (1993). Loss and mourning: Milestones in theory, research and treatment. In R. Malkinson, S. Rubin, & E. Vitzom (Eds.), [*Loss and mourning in the Israeli society*] (pp. 21–38). Jerusalem: Cana and Ministry of Defense. *Ovdan Ushchol Bechevra HaIsraelit*

Rubin, S. (1994). In M. S. Stroebe, W. Stroebe, & R. O. Hansson (Eds.), *Handbook of bereavement: Theory, research, and intervention* (pp. 285–299). Cambridge, England: Cambridge University Press.

Rynearson, E. K., & McCreery, J. M. (1993). Bereavement after homicide: A synergism of trauma and loss. *American Journal of Psychiatry, 150*(2), 258–261.

Sanders, C. M. (1986). Accidental death of a child. In T. A. Rando (Ed.), *Parental loss of a child* (pp. 181–191). Champaign, IL: Research Press.

Sanders, C. M. (1992). *How to survive the loss of a child: Filling the emptiness and rebuilding your life*. Rocklin, CA: Prima.

Schaefer, D., & Lyons, C. (1988). *How do we tell the children?* New York: New Market Press.

Schatz, B. D. (1986). Grief of mothers. In T. A. Rando (Ed.), *Parental loss of a child* (pp. 303–315). Champaign, IL: Research Press.

Schiff, S. H. (1977). *The bereaved parent*. New York: Penguin.

Schneider, J. (1984). *Stress, loss and grief*. Baltimore: University Park Press.

Schneider, J. M. (1994). *Finding my way*. Colfax, WI: Seasons.

Schneur Zalman of Liadi. (1984). *Likutei Amarim. Tanya*. New York: Kehot Publication Society. (Original work published 1797)

Schochet, J. I. (1990a). *The mystical tradition*. New York: Kehot Publication Society.

Schochet, J. I. (1990b). *Deep calling unto deep*. New York: Kehot Publication Society.

Schochet, J. I. (1990c). *Chassidic dimensions*. New York: Kehot Publication Society.

Schochet, J. I. (1988). *Mystical concepts in Chassidism*. New York: Kehot Publication Society.

Scholem, G. G. (1961). *Major trends in Jewish mysticism*. New York: Schocken.

Shapiro, E. R. (1994). *Grief as a family process. A developmental approach to clinical practice*. New York: Guilford.

Shilony, E., & Grossman, F. K. (1993). Depersonalization as a defense mechanism in survivors of trauma. *Journal of Traumatic Stress, 6*(1), 119–128.

Sperr, E. V., Sperr, S. J., Craft, R. B., & Boudewyns, P. A. (1990). MMPI profiles and post-traumatic symptomology in former prisoners of war. *Journal of Traumatic Stress, 3*(3), 369–378.

Spiegel, Y. (1977). *The grief process: Analysis and counseling.* Nashville, TN: Abingdon.

Sprang, G., & McNeil, J. S. (1995). *The many faces of bereavement: The nature and treatment of natural, traumatic, and stigmatized grief.* New York: Brunner/Mazel.

Sprang, M. V., McNeil, J. S., & Wright, R. (1989). Psychological changes after the murder of a significant other. *Social Casework, 70*(3), 159–164.

Staudacher, C. (1991). *Men and grief.* Oakland, CA: New Harbinger Publications.

Stroebe, M. S. (1993). Coping with bereavement: A review of the grief work hypothesis. *Omega: Journal of Death and Dying, 26*(1), 19–42.

Stroebe, M. S., Gergen, M. M., Gergen, K. J., Stroebe, W., Kelly, J. D., Klass, D., Silverman, P. R., Nickman, S., & Worden, J. W. (1995). The experience of grief. In L. A. DeSpelder & A. L. Strickland (Eds.), *The path ahead: Readings in death and dying* (pp. 231–270). Mountain View, CA: Mayfield.

Stroebe, M. S., Stroebe, W., & Hansson, R. O. (Eds.). (1994). *Handbook of bereavement: Theory, research, and intervention.* Cambridge, England: Cambridge University Press.

Sylvia, C. (1997). *A change of heart: A memoir.* Boston: Little, Brown.

Tamir, G. (1993). Long-term adjustment of war bereaved parents in Israel. In R. Malkinson, S. Rubin, & E. Vitzom (Eds.), *Ovdan Ushchol Bechevra HaIsraelit* [Loss and mourning in the Israeli society]. Jerusalem: Cana and Ministry of Defense.

Thoits, P. A. (1983). Multiple identities and psychological well-being: A reformulation and test of the social isolation hypothesis. *American Sociological Review, 48,* 174–187.

Trickett, P. K., & Putnam, F. W. (1993). Impact of child sexual abuse on females: Toward a developmental, psychobiological integration. *Psychological Science, 4*(2), 81–87.

Vacc, N. A., DeVaney, S. B., & Wittmer, J. (Eds.). (1995). *Experiencing and counseling multicultural and diverse populations.* Bristol, PA: Accelerated Development.

van-der-Kolk, B. A., & Fisler, R. E. (1994). Childhood abuse and neglect and loss of self-regulation. *Bulletin of the Menninger Clinic, 58*(2), 145–168.

Volkan, V. D. (1983). *Linking objects and linking phenomena.* New York: International Universities Press.

Wass, H. (1984). Parents, teachers, and health professionals as helpers. In H. Wass & C. A. Corr (Eds.), *Helping children cope with death* (pp. 75–133). New York: Hemisphere.

Wass, H., & Corr, C. A. (1984). *Childhood and death.* Washington, DC: Hemisphere.

Webb, N. B. (1993). The child and death. In N. B. Webb (Ed.), *Helping bereaved children: A handbook for practitioners* (pp. 3–18). New York: Guilford.

Weinberg, N. (1994). Self-blame, other-blame, and desire for revenge: Factors in recovery from bereavement. *Death Studies, 18*(6), 583–593.

Wessel, M. A. (1984). Helping families: Thoughts of a pediatrician. In H. Wass & C. A. Corr (Eds.), *Childhood and death* (pp. 205–216). Washington, DC: Hemisphere.

Wheeler, I. (1994). The role of meaning and purpose in life in bereaved parents associated with a self-help group: Compassionate friends. *Omega: Journal of Death and Dying, 28*(4), 261–271.

Wolfelt, A. (1994). *Helping children cope with grief.* Bristol, PA: Accelerated Development.

Worden, J. W. (1991). *Grief counseling and grief therapy: A handbook for the mental health practitioner* (2nd ed.). New York: Springer.

Worden, J. W., & Monahan, J. R. (1993). Caring for bereaved parents. In A. Armstrong-Dailey & S. Goltzer (Eds.), *Hospice care for children* (pp. 122–139). New York: Oxford University Press.

Zakowski, S., Hall, M. H., & Baum, A. (1992). Stress, stress management, and the immune system. *Applied and Preventive Psychology, 1*(1), 1–13.

Zisook, S., Schuchter, S. R., Irwin, M., Darko, D. F., Sledge, P., & Resovsky, K. (1994). Bereavement, depression, and immune function. *Psychiatry Research, 52*(1), 1–10.

ORGANIZATIONS AND OTHER RESOURCES

The Compassionate Friends National Headquarters
P.O. Box 3696
Oak Brook, IL 60522–3696
(708) 990–0010

The Candlelighters Childhood Cancer Foundation
1901 Pennsylvania Avenue, NW, Suite 1001
Washington, DC 20006
(202) 659–5136

Mothers Against Drunk Driving (MADD)
669 Airport Freeway, Suite 310
Hurst, TX 76053
(817) 268–6233

National Sudden Infant Death Syndrome (SIDS) Foundation
8200 Professional Place, Suite 104
Landover, MD 20785
(800) 221–SIDS

National SIDS Clearinghouse
8201 Greenboro Drive, Suite 600
McLean, VA 22102
(703) 821–8955

Parents of Murdered Children (POMC)
100 East 8th Street, B-41
Cincinnati, OH 45202
(800) 327–2499, ext. 4288
Emergencies (513) 721–5683

The Pregnancy and Infant Loss Center
1421 East Wayzata Boulevard
Wayzata, MN 55391
(612) 473–9372

Index

About the Author

Dr. Henya Kagan (Klein) is a licensed and certified psychologist in Texas. She has been working as a psychologist for more than twenty years both in Israel and in the United States. She has provided direct service to adults and children who suffered from a large range of problems, and has taught and published in various areas. Her specialty in recent years has become that of bereavement, and adjustment to loss. Henya Kagan (Klein) is a relocated Israeli in the United States since 1981. Born in Europe, she grew up in Israel and served in the Israeli army. Her remaining family lives in Israel.

On December 29, 1989, her 11-year-old daughter, Gili Klein, was fatally injured by a reckless driver. Five days later, on January 3, 1990, she died. On May 20, 1994, her husband, Prof. Norman Kagan, died of lung cancer.

Dr. Kagan (Klein) is a graduate of Psychology from Bar-Ilan University, Israel, and of Counseling Psychology from the University of Illinois at Urbana-Champaign, where she received her Ph.D. In her last professional positions in Israel, she worked as the director of one of the largest rehabilitation centers in the country and as a psychologist at a municipal psychological services center. In the United States, since receiving her doctorate, she has been a professor at the University of Georgia at Athens and the University of Houston–Clear Lake. She currently devotes most of her time to bereaved people in her private practice in Houston, and does consultation, research, and writing on bereavement.